THE
SERVANT-MESSIAH

A Study of the Public Ministry of Jesus

BY

T. W. MANSON, D.D.

Rylands Professor of Biblical Criticism and Exegesis
University of Manchester
Fellow of the British Academy

Baker Book House
Grand Rapids, Michigan

First published in 1953
Paperback edition issued 1977 by
Baker Book House
with permission of Cambridge University Press
ISBN: 0-8010-6012-5

Foreword © 1977 by
Baker Book House

First printing, March 1977
Second printing, September 1980
Third printing, June 1984

PHOTOLITHOPRINTED BY CUSHING - MALLOY, INC.
ANN ARBOR, MICHIGAN, UNITED STATES OF AMERICA

FOREWORD

F. F. Bruce

The contents of *The Servant Messiah* is based on two lecture courses given by T. W. Manson (1893-1958) — the Shaffer Lectures in Yale Divinity School in 1939 and a course delivered in the University of Cambridge in 1951.

When Professor Manson chose the messianic ministry of Jesus as the theme for these two lecture courses, he chose a subject he knew well. *The Teaching of Jesus,* published in 1931, had immediately established him as a leader in the world of New Testament scholarship. In it he made a valuable contribution to the discussion of the significance of the Kingdom of God and the Son of Man in Jesus' thought. And he expounded this contribution afresh in simple terms in *The Servant Messiah.* It is unfashionable today to hold, as Professor Manson did, that Jesus understood the Son of Man in terms of the Isaianic Servant of the Lord. But unfashionable as it is, Professor Manson's arguments for it are completely convincing.

The Servant Messiah sets forth the principles and practice of Jesus' ministry against the background of the messianic hope from Jeremiah to John the Baptist. Professor Manson shows how Jesus' death, far from interrupting His ministry, crowned it and, together with His resurrection, guaranteed its continuation on a world-wide scale. Professor Manson explains that the people of Christ do not *inherit* their task from Christ, they *share* it with Him; they are not His successors but His companions, participants in the corporate identity of the Son of Man.

Professor Manson was fully aware of the danger of tackling this subject—the danger of reconstituting Jesus in one's own image or of seeing one's own ideals embodied in Jesus' life and teaching. But Professor Manson was the man who coined the frequently repeated warning: "By their Lives of Jesus ye shall know them." By recognizing the danger, he was the better able to avoid it. He manifested a rare insight into the quintessence of Jesus' teaching; at the same time his appraisal of it is marked by historical objectivity. Professor Manson taught that the distinctiveness of Jesus' teaching is the more clearly appreciated when it is viewed in its historical context. However, with one aspect of that context Professor Manson did not greatly concern himself: he professed skepticism about "the nutritious properties of Dead Sea fruit." This was not because he could not come to terms with the Qumran scrolls, but because he did not find them as relevant to his subject as some of his colleagues imagined them to be in the first excitement of their discovery.

Much has been written about the life and ministry of Jesus since this little book appeared in 1953 but it remains, in my judgment, one of the most trustworthy guides to this important subject that is available today.

For the last twenty-two years of his life, T. W. Manson was Rylands Professor of Biblical Criticism and Exegesis in the University of Manchester (England).

University of Manchester

April 1976

PREFACE

THIS short book has a longish history. It began with an invitation to give the Shaffer Lectures for 1939 at Yale University Divinity School. The lectures were given in the spring of that year; and I wish to record my gratitude for the honour of being asked to give them and for much kindness, then and since, from the members of the Faculty and especially from the Dean, now Dean Emeritus, Dr L. A. Weigle.

The outbreak of the Second World War, and the new and heavy tasks which it brought, prevented me from publishing the lectures at that time; and the manuscript remained with other papers, receiving additions and modifications from time to time.

In the Michaelmas Term of 1951 I gave a short course of lectures in the University of Cambridge taking as my subject the Messianic Ministry, and using as a basis the material which I had originally prepared for the Shaffer Lectures, and later revised and expanded. It is this Cambridge revised version of the original Yale lectures that is printed in the pages that follow. I am grateful to the Divinity Board of the University of Cambridge for the invitation to lecture, and particularly to my old friend Professor R. D. Whitehorn of Westminster College for constant kindness and generous hospitality while the lecturing was in progress.

I have to thank my secretary, Miss K. M. Whiteley, for preparing the typescript, and the officials and craftsmen of the University Press for their skill and care in the printing.

T. W. M.

UNIVERSITY OF MANCHESTER
November 1952

CONTENTS

CONIVGI
DILECTISSIMAE

CHAPTER I

THE MESSIANIC HOPE

T HE genealogy of the third Gospel and the Prologue to the fourth alike carry the history of Jesus back to the beginning of the history of the world and man. The first Gospel and the Apocalypse visualize the continuation of the story until history is wound up. While it is certainly true that the philosopher and the theologian cannot be content with anything but the most comprehensive view, the historian must needs be more modest and content himself, and if possible his readers, with the survey of a more restricted field. For our purposes the fences may be erected at 63 B.C., the date of the capture of Jerusalem by Pompey, and A.D. 70, the date of the destruction of the city by Titus; but it is certain that we shall have to look over the fences, particularly the former, from time to time, and occasionally to step outside.

One major result of a still earlier fall of Jerusalem in 586 B.C. was that the life of the Hebrew people was given a new focus and orientation: what we call Judaism began to grow up. It was Judaism that first actualised the idea of a religious community within a political order that does not share the same faith, and of the local congregation (the Synagogue) within the larger community.[1] This was the logical issue of the process described by Skinner[2] in the religious experience of Jeremiah. Religion ends by being the concern of religious individuals, who together form a religious community, the religious life of which goes on whatever the political, social and economic environment may happen to be.

But the genius of Hebrew and Jewish religion could not

---

[1] F. Loofs, *Dogmengeschichte*⁵, pp. 28 f.
[2] *Prophecy and Religion*, chs. XI and XVI–XVIII.

rest in this divorce of 'sacred' and 'secular'. The world must be brought into line with the Church. The ideals taught in the Synagogue must be realised in the national life. The unity between the political and the spiritual life of Israel which had been violently broken by the catastrophes of 721 and 586 B.C. must be restored. The religious soul of Israel must find a body. Hence the Messianic hope, the hope of restoring on a higher level the unity of national life that had been broken at the Exile.[1] The faith and hope of Israel found expression in the Apocalypses. Here was the vision. The rule of life, the foundations on which the new order must be built, the tasks and responsibilities of Israel—all this was included in God's directions to Israel, and under three main heads as laid down by Simeon the Righteous[2] in the third century B.C.: the God-given Law of Moses, the divinely ordained ritual of the Temple, and the day-to-day expression, in acts of mutual kindness and helpfulness, of the corporate solidarity of the covenant people.

Along with the demand for the reintegration of the present life of Israel went the hardly less urgent call for the re-establishment of continuity with Israel's past. In fact the latter turned out to be the condition of the former: the unity of the nation's life was re-established on the basis of the nation's traditions. The covenant made with the Fathers was the only sure foundation on which to build. The Rule of Faith and the Rule of Life were there in its terms, in the commandments, the statutes, the judgements, in the immemorial ritual of the Temple. The Law and the Worship were Israel's unbreakable link with her past. When the Torah was read, she could hear the echo of the thunders that had once rolled round the summit of Sinai.[3] When the father of a

[1] See H. H. Rowley, *The Relevance of Apocalyptic*, pp. 14 ff.
[2] *Aboth* i. 2.
[3] This demand for continuity and reliance on tradition is not peculiar to Judaism. We have a similar phenomenon in the history of Greek Philosophy,

Jewish family offered his passover lamb in the Temple he felt himself linked by the ritual with his ancestors whom God had liberated from the Egyptian bondage.

It was these things that held the Jewish people together through many a dark and tragic period in their history: it was these things that were to be gloriously vindicated in the good time that was coming. When we speak of the Messianic hope, we are not to think of a philosophical theory such as is embodied in the *Republic* or Aristotle's *Ethics* and *Politics*. The Messianic hope was a burning conviction held with fanatical zeal, shaped under pressure of tyranny and persecution, and inspired by deep religious faith. It had to be, if it was to stand up to the strain and stress of the period from Daniel to Akiba. To that we now turn. Antiochus IV Epiphanes ascended the throne of the Seleucid Empire in the winter of 176–175 B.C.; the final revolt of the Jews under Hadrian broke out in A.D. 132 and came to its inevitable and bloody end in A.D. 135. That period of just over three centuries may fairly be called the period of the Jewish fight for freedom. It opens with the Maccabean struggle and the rule of the Hasmonean dynasty. The Hasmoneans reached the zenith of their power and prosperity in the reign of Alexander Jannaeus, king and high priest (103–76 B.C.). On the death of his widow in 67 B.C., the power of the dynasty swiftly declined: the decline was hastened by internal feuds as well as by intrigues from without. In 63 B.C. came the end of Jewish independence with the conquest by Pompey: Hyrcanus II and Antigonus, who continued the dynasty till 37 B.C., were no more than puppet rulers exercising limited powers in a reduced territory under

the so-called *Successions of the Philosophers* (cf. Dudley, *History of Cynicism*, p. 4; Hicks, *Diogenes Laertius*, Introd. p. xxiv). And it is perhaps significant that the growth of traditionalism in Greek philosophy is roughly contemporary with the similar development in Judaism. It is interesting to compare the pedigree given by Diogenes Laertius (i. 14; set out by Dudley, *op. cit.* p. 215) with the corresponding Jewish chain of tradition in Aboth i. On tradition see further below, pp. 18 ff.

1-2

the watchful eye of the Roman Governor of Syria, or else, from 49 B.C. onwards, pawns in the game of Roman power-politicians. The year 30 B.C. saw the recognition of Herod by Augustus as king, under Roman suzerainty, a ruler as distasteful to the Jews as he was tolerable to the Romans. With the death of Herod (4 B.C.) direct Roman control tended to increase, and with it the discontent of the ardently patriotic section of the people. A number of abortive risings, easily suppressed, paved the way for the great revolt of A.D. 66–70, so vividly described by Josephus. But that was not the end. There was another rising of Jews in Egypt, Cyrene, Cyprus and Mesopotamia in the reign of Trajan (A.D. 115–17) and the last vain struggle under the leadership of Bar Cochba (A.D. 132–5). Three centuries of struggle against overwhelming odds.

The Ministry of Jesus falls at the end of the second of these three centuries, when the Jews of Palestine had still the memory of the Maccabean triumphs and no foreknowledge of the horrors of the siege under Titus; when it might still be argued that what had happened to the house of Seleucus could equally happen to the dynasty founded by Augustus, and that Jewish patriotism backed by divine power might deal with a Tiberius as faithfully as it had once dealt with Antiochus Epiphanes. It is on *that* background that the Ministry must be understood: the context in which the Synoptic Gospels are to be read will be provided by such books as Daniel, I and II Maccabees, the Psalms of Solomon, and the *Jewish War* of Josephus.[1]

It is, however, necessary to state rather carefully what we mean by 'the Jewish fight for freedom', and in particular

---

[1] An illuminating side-light on the subject is cast by the opening words of Eus. *H.E.* IV, 6 (describing the Hadrianic war), καὶ δῆτα τῆς 'Ιουδαίων ἀποστασίας αὖθις εἰς μέγα καὶ πολὺ προελθούσης....The situation as Eusebius sees it is not one of alternate periods of submission and revolt, but of perpetual disaffection, shortly called ἡ 'Ιουδαίων ἀποστασία, which periodically breaks out into open and violent resistance.

I should suggest that we make a mistake when we define the struggle in terms of 'religious' freedom or 'political' freedom. Throughout this period the Jews were fighting, not for such modern ideals as these,[1] but for the life of 'Israel', where 'Israel' is a complex organic whole which includes the monotheistic faith, the cultus in Temple and Synagogue, the law and custom embodied in the Torah, the political institutions which had grown up in the post-exilic period, the claim to ownership of the Holy Land, and whatever dreams there may have been of an Israelite world-rule to supersede the rule of the Gentile empires. For the Jew this cause of Israel was a single and indivisible thing. Different aspects of it, different elements in it, might be more prominent in the interest and affection of different sections of Jewry, but no Jew could shake himself entirely free from any part of the complex inheritance. There is abundant evidence not only in Jewish sources, but also in the New Testament itself, that devotion to the cause of Israel was the dominant factor in the common life of Palestinian Jews before, during, and after the Ministry of Jesus; and I shall continually invoke it to explain outstanding events and critical decisions in the Ministry itself. For the moment I content myself with a single example taken from Luke, who of all the evangelists is least open to the charge of Jewish chauvinism.

[1] The Jews were not specially interested in 'religious freedom' if that means the right of the individual to determine by his own reason and conscience his religious beliefs and practices. On the contrary, the Maccabees took up arms against such a view. They fought for the principle that no religion whatever should be tolerated on Jewish soil except the religion of Judaism. The first blow struck in the Maccabean Revolt, by the aged father of Judas Maccabaeus and his brothers, is against *a Jew* who is about to conform to the heathen cult: I Macc. ii. 23 f. 'A Jew came forward in the sight of all to sacrifice upon the altar in Modin in accordance with the King's command. And when Mattathias saw it, his zeal was kindled, and his heart quivered (with wrath); and his indignation burst forth according to the judgement (κατὰ τὸ κρίμα, i.e. the judgement passed by God on conduct of this kind and set forth in the Law: see Deut. xii. 1; xiii. 1–11; xvii. 2–7), so that he ran and slew him by the altar.' So much for religious freedom!

The opening chapters of his gospel are frequently set before us as an idyllic picture of the simple gentle piety of the ordinary godly Jew who belonged to none of the recognised 'sects' or 'parties' in Judaism. We hear the *Magnificat* chanted in church and the mental picture accompanying the words and music is that of the Madonna and Child. But let us look again at the sentiments expressed in this *berceuse*:

With his own arm he has wrought mightily;
He has routed the arrogant, for all their scheming.
He has deposed rulers from their thrones,
And exalted the humble:
He has given the hungry their fill of good things;
But the rich he has sent away with nothing.
Once more in his mercy he has taken the part of Israel his servant;
As he promised to our forefathers, to Abraham and his descendants
for ever. (Luke i. 51–5)

Similar ideas are expressed by the good old priest Zacharias:

Blessed be the Lord the God of Israel,
For he has watched over his people and wrought redemption for
them,
And raised up the agent of our deliverance from among the
descendants of his servant David...
As he promised long ago in the declarations of his holy prophets...
A deliverance from our enemies and from the control of those who
hate us;
To deal mercifully with our fathers, and to be mindful of his holy
covenant,
The oath which he swore to our father Abraham, that he would
give us
Freedom from fear and from the control of our enemies, so that
we should worship him in holiness and righteousness, remaining
in his presence our whole life long. (Luke i. 68–75)

I find it difficult to believe that Luke, one of whose tendencies is to represent Christianity as politically innocuous, could have composed these pieces himself. It seems more likely that he

6

has preserved for us traditional material which really indicates the hopes and desires of the stratum of Jewish society in which Christianity was cradled.

We may look at the background of the Ministry from another point of view. Josephus, in the *Antiquities* (XII, 138–53), gives certain documents from the time of Antiochus the Great issued when the Jewish state was in favour with the Seleucid court (*c.* 200 B.C.).[1] From these we learn of three large concessions made to the Jews by Antiochus.

(*a*) The hereditary laws—i.e. those embodied in the Pentateuch—are declared to be binding on all members of the Jewish community.[2]

(*b*) A royal contribution is made towards the cost of the Temple worship.[3]

(*c*) Members of the *Gerousia* (the Jewish Senate of the time), the Temple priesthood and choir, and the 'Temple scribes' are exempted from the poll-tax, the crown-tax, and the salt-tax.

At first sight it seems a good thing that the institutions of Judaism are recognised by, and put under the patronage of, a great king. But such benefits are apt to be illusory. The royal recognition of the high priest and his retinue soon

[1] On these documents see Eduard Meyer, *Ursprung und Anfänge des Christentums*, II, 127, n. 2; R. Marcus, *Josephus* (Loeb Library), VII, 743–66 (with a full bibliography, 743 f.).

[2] This may not be the first time that the Jewish Law had come under Gentile patronage: for there is the possibility that Ezra's promulgation of the Law was backed by Persian authority and power. See *Law and Religion* (ed. E. I. J. Rosenthal), p. 55, n. 3. For the triumph of the opposite tendency in Islam see H. A. R. Gibb in *Law and Religion*, pp. 153 f. 'The Law was laid down by jurists independent of either Caliph or Sultan, and often in opposition to them. It had merely to be formulated by the Jurists to become valid, it had no need of formal promulgation by the civil authorities, nor could the Caliph deny its validity, though he might not always act in accordance with it' (p. 154).

[3] According to II Macc. iii. 1–3 the payment was continued by Seleucus IV Philopator. It is possible that earlier still, in the Persian period, royal contributions had been made to the Sacrifices of the Second Temple: see Ezra vi. 9 (with Bertholet's notes, *KHC ad loc.*); vii. 17 ff. Further details of the participation of Gentile rulers in the Jerusalem cultus in Schürer, *GJV*⁴, II, 357–63; Finkelstein, *The Pharisees*, II, 682 f.

comes to mean that there can be no high priest without the royal recognition: and so it comes about that the high priest who, in theory, is invested by God 'with authority over statute and judgement, that he may teach his people statutes and judgements unto the children of Israel' (Ecclus. xlv. 17), is in fact nominated by a heathen monarch and holds his job on condition of being the king's 'yes-man'.[1] Similarly, a royal contribution to the cultus soon gives place to the attempt to exercise a royal control over the cultus. Finally, as Bickermann well points out, there is a glaring contradiction involved in the very idea that the statutory force of the Torah should depend on the consent of a Gentile ruler. The later actions of Antiochus Epiphanes have their precedent in this antinomy, that a theocracy (a kingdom of God) is established on the basis of the decree of an earthly lord who knows little and cares less about the deity who is presumed to rule over this 'kingdom of God'.[2] That is to say, the fundamental affirmations of Judaism were denied by the patronage of Antiochus III as really as by the persecutions of Antiochus IV. That the former should confirm the crown rights of Jehovah was just as much *lèse-majesté* as that the latter should deny them. So, for any sensitive Jewish spirit the affront of Gentile overlordship was present and real, humiliating and sacrilegious, whether the Gentile overlord were tolerant or the reverse. There is no reason to think that Jewish resentment at the affront weakened at any time during the three centuries with which we are concerned. We have thus to reckon with the fact that any thinking Jew in this period might quite reasonably look upon armed revolt against the foreigner not merely as a patriotic act, but also as a religious protest against insult offered to Almighty God. A war for Jewish freedom was also a holy war, a war for the kingdom of God.

[1] Cf. E. Bickermann, *Der Gott der Makkabäer*, p. 58.
[2] Bickermann, *op. cit.* p. 53.

This consideration is important in view of the assertion that used to be made—and still crops up occasionally—that Jewish Messianic ideals were 'materialistic' or 'purely political' or 'this-worldly'. The kind of Jew who had Messianic ideals in this period did not make these abstractions. He believed in a God who was actively participating in the course of history: and consequently he saw himself as a subject of this divine king here and now. If he took up arms against the unclean Gentile, it was not just a political move: it was also a religious undertaking. The campaigns of Israel could be regarded quite naturally as the wars of Jehovah. Where the whole activity of man from the cradle to the grave is taken into the ambit of his religion, there is no place left for the 'purely political' or the 'merely materialistic'.[1]

That phrase 'the kingdom of God' seems to introduce a new and complicating factor into the problem; but it need not, if we are willing to put ourselves at the standpoint of the average God-fearing and patriotic Jew of the time. He knew what he meant when he spoke of fighting for Israel: and Israel was the concrete manifestation of the purpose of God in history. The Torah of Israel was God's declared will, the Temple worship the ordained means of approach to him, the High Priest his chosen representative. The fuller and richer and more effective the life of Israel, the more truly the will of God was fulfilled in the world. If Israel could be one hundred per cent Israel, enjoying all the privileges and shouldering all

---

[1] To say this is not in any way to minimise the importance of economic conditions in Palestine at the beginning of our era, especially the very heavy burden of the double taxation, ecclesiastical and civil. (On this see F. C. Grant, *The Economic Background of the Gospels*; J. Jeremias, *Jerusalem zur Zeit Jesu*, I and IIA; J. Juster, *Les Juifs dans l'Empire Romain*, II, 280–326; E. Schürer, *Geschichte des Judischen Volkes*[4], I, 473–9, ii, 297–317; L. Finkelstein, *J.B.L.* XLIX, 32–7.) But it must be remembered that economics was not regarded as lying outside the scope of the Torah, and that the establishment of the reign of God had its economic aspect. Economic justice was in Jewish eyes included in God's purpose: since the days of Amos and Isaiah it had been a religious issue as really as prayer and sacrifice.

the responsibilities of their position, the purpose of God would be realised: the kingdom of God would be a reality. Theologically the implications of that might go very deep, touching questions of predestination, providence, free will, of angelology and demonology and the like. But for the average Jew the remembering of the Covenant by God, the performance of the promise made to the Patriarchs, in other words the establishment of the kingdom of God, meant 'freedom from fear and from the control of our enemies; so that we should worship him in holiness and righteousness, remaining in his presence our whole life long'. It meant complete Jewish autonomy with Temple and Torah here and now. I should not argue that there is nothing else in the Jewish hope of the future as it was cherished in this period; but I do maintain, that any exposition that does not recognise the great, I should say decisive, part played by this simple concrete 'practical' programme cannot begin to do justice to the facts presented in the Gospels.

It may seem that we are giving too much attention to the views of the 'average Jew', the 'man in the street' of Jerusalem or Capernaum. We ought to give more attention to him; if only because there were more of him than of any other kind of Jew in the period with which we are concerned. Probably most, if not all, of the Twelve were 'average Jews': certainly the vast majority in the crowds that gathered round Jesus were. We are not so well instructed about their beliefs and hopes as we are about those of smaller but more influential bodies, and we have constantly to remind ourselves that those influential bodies constituted only a small fraction of the population of Palestine. Josephus puts the number of Pharisees in the time of Herod the Great at about 6000,[1]

---

[1] *Ant.* XVII, 2, 4, §42. See the discussion of the figures by Jeremias, *Jerusalem*, IIB, 122. It is probable that Josephus is here dependent on Nicholas of Damascus, who was, by his position at Herod's court, likely to be accurately informed on such matters as this.

In estimating the numbers of the Pharisees in Palestine we must bear in and that is the figure for the whole extent of Herod's territory. To the Essenes he gives a total membership of 4000,[1] while for the Sadducees he gives no precise figures, telling us only that the members of the party are few.[2] The important point is that the Pharisees, Sadducees and Essenes together can hardly have amounted to more than 30,000–35,000 persons, whereas the population of Jerusalem alone may be put at not less than 55,000–95,000 to say nothing of the Jews in the Judaean countryside and in the territory of Herod Antipas. Jeremias estimated the total Jewish population of Palestine in the time of Jesus at 500,000–600,000.[3] If he is right, the Pharisees were 5 per cent of the population, and Pharisees, Sadducees, and Essenes together perhaps 7 per cent; the other 93 per cent were presumably 'average Jews'.

Nevertheless, we must not neglect the 7 per cent, for though few they were influential. Even the Essenes, who withdrew from the ordinary life of the time into a monastic seclusion, had still an appeal strong enough to maintain their numbers by recruits from outside, which was the only way by which they could continue to exist as a society. They are the least important of the three groups for our purpose; for it is of the essence of their doctrine that they are separated from the world. Indeed, if the commonly accepted etymology of the name Pharisee were correct—which I do not believe—the Essenes would have had a far better title to it than the Pharisees themselves.[4]

mind that full membership of the Pharisaic Communities (*haburoth*) was open only to males, and probably only to those who had reached years of discretion. What the minimum age was we do not know; but in any case a large proportion of the members will have been heads of families and it may be presumed that their families would be under Pharisaic influence and that their womenfolk would be adherents of Pharisaism. We should probably be safe in estimating the total number of persons closely connected with the movement as members or adherents at about 25,000. It is probable that a large proportion of these were concentrated in Jerusalem, perhaps as many as 20,000.

[1] *Ant.* XVIII, I, 5.   [2] *Ant.* XVIII, I, 4.
[3] *Jerusalem*, IIB, 68.
[4] For the little that is known about the Essenes see Schürer, *G.J.V.*[4], II, 651–80 (where there is a full bibliography of the literature up to 1906);

The Sadducees were important not by reason of their numbers (they were a small and very select body) or their place in popular esteem (the mass of the people followed the lead of the Pharisees, so far as they followed any lead at all), but by the fact that they held the highest offices in Church and State. They are not to be simply identified with the priesthood, though many of them belonged to the upper ranks of the hierarchy.[1] Nor was the Sadducean group composed exclusively of members of the priestly aristocracy: Jeremias has shown[2] that there was a lay aristocracy which should most probably be included. In the *Bulletin of the John Rylands Library*, XXII (1938), 144–59 I argued that the generally accepted explanation of the name Sadducee, which connects it with Ṣadoḳ (Zadok), the high priest of Solomon's reign,[3] is untenable on historical and philological grounds.

The historical objection may be put in this way. The high priests of the period 172 B.C. to A.D. 70 were, with two exceptions (Ananel[4] 37 B.C. and Phineas A.D. 67 (68)–70) not of Zadokite descent at all. In 170/169 B.C. the legitimate Zadokite high priestly dynasty transferred its activities to Egypt and there founded a rival sanctuary at Leontopolis. Menelaus (172–162 B.C.), if he was a priest at all, belonged to the priestly tribe of Bilgah; Alcimus (162–160 B.C.) was a non-Zadokite priest. From 160 to 152 B.C. the office was vacant, and in the latter year, at the Feast of Tabernacles, Jonathan

---

Juster, *Les Juifs dans l'Empire Romain*, I, 487–92; W. Bauer, art. 'Essener' in Pauly-Wissowa, *R.E.*, Suppl. IV, cols. 386–430; J. Thomas, *Le Mouvement Baptiste en Palestine et Syrie*, pp. 1–32.

[1] The total number of priests and levites in the time of Jesus is estimated by Jeremias (*Jerusalem*, IIB, 66) at about 18,000. The Sadducees were a small group.　　　　[2] *Jerusalem*, IIB, 88–100.

[3] On the history of this hypothesis see L. Finkelstein, *The Pharisees*, II, 663, n. 20: 'The derivation of the name Sadducee from that of the High Priest Zadok was first proposed by Geiger, *Urschrift*, p. 100.' That is to say, the Sadducees themselves do not appear to have laid claim to the Zadokite affiliation. Zadok the high priest was fathered on them in the early nineteenth century. Their own explanation of their name was quite different. See below, p. 16, n. 2.

[4] Jeremias, *Jerusalem*, IIB, 53 f.

Maccabaeus began the long line of the Hasmonean high priests, the last of whom, Aristobulus, held office in 35 B.C. Of the twenty-eight high priests between 37 B.C. and A.D. 70 Ananel and Phineas were Zadokites, Aristobulus was a Hasmonean, and the rest were all from families belonging to the rank and file of the priesthood.

The upshot of the matter is that from 170 B.C. onwards the genuine Zadokite priesthood was not in Palestine at all, having migrated to Leontopolis. It follows that, on the ordinary interpretation of 'Sadducee', the name must have been in common use before this date. But Josephus makes the first mention of Sadducees in the high priesthood of Jonathan Maccabaeus[1] (152–143 B.C.). In other words, when we have a Zadokite high priesthood, we have no mention of the Sadducees, and when the Sadducees appear on the scene, there are no more Zadokite high priests. Moreover, if Jeremias is right in maintaining that the Sadducees were a mixed group of priests and wealthy laymen, the derivation of the name from Ṣadok *the priest* becomes less likely than ever. The philological difficulties in the way of connecting the word Sadducee with the same Ṣadok are discussed in the article referred to above.

Before going on to offer an explanation of the name Sadducee which seems to avoid these difficulties, it may be well to reiterate some points which are well enough known but not always well enough remembered in discussing the Sadducees.

(i) The Sadducees are not to be identified simply with the priesthood.[2] The Sadducees were a small group: the priests numbered over 7000, and the priests and levites together

---

[1] *Ant.* XIII, 5, 9.

[2] Many priests were Pharisees: Josephus himself (*Vita*, 1 f., 12); Hananiah, 'prefect of the priests'; R. Jose the Priest, a disciple of Johanan b. Zakkai. See further Jeremias, *Jerusalem*, IIB, 127 ff. We may note also the observance of Synagogue ritual in the Temple (Mishnah, *Tamid* IV, 3; V, 1). Cf. L. Finkelstein, *The Pharisees*, I, 62 ff.; Jeremias, *Jerusalem*, IIA, 19.

about 18,000. Again, the Sadducees were not all priests: the party appears to have been composed of a relatively small number of priests connected with the higher posts in the Temple service, together with members of the lay aristocracy.

(ii) In matters of religion the leading characteristic of the Sadducees is a determined resistance to all innovations; and, while stubborn conservatism is a common enough ecclesiastical phenomenon, it is not the stuff of which new sects are made. The matter has been well put by Meyer: 'So halten auch bei den Juden die besitzenden Klassen in Staat und Kirche an den alten Anschauungen fest und wollen von den Neuerungen nichts wissen. Aber eben dadurch sind sie zur Stagnation und schliesslich zum Absterben verurteilt; es fehlt ihnen ein lebendiges, schöpferisches Prinzip, sie können lediglich negieren.'[1]

(iii) While the religious position of the Sadducees has to be defined in terms of the doctrines which they rejected, the positive characteristics of the party belong to another sphere. They are the wealthy (εὔποροι)[2] and the people of high social standing (πρῶτοι τοῖς ἀξιώμασιν).[3] Their manners are stiff to the point of rudeness, and that even among themselves.[4] In the administration of justice they are harsh and severe.[5] These traits are all well known, and it is important to keep them in mind. The positive qualities of the Sadducees are just those most likely to be developed in a class that has had the responsibilities and the opportunities of political leadership in a period of almost continuous political crisis.

---

[1] *Ursprung und Anfänge des Christentums*, II, 293 f. Cf. J. Z. Lauterbach in *Hebrew Union College Annual*, VI (1929), 77.

[2] Josephus, *Ant.* XIII, 298.

[3] *Ant.* XVIII, 17. For the force of ἀξίωμα here, we may compare *Monumentum Ancyranum*, 34, 3: ἀξιώματι πάντων διήνεγκα, where ἀξιώματι renders the Latin *auctoritate.*   [4] Josephus, *B.J.* II, 166.

[5] *Ant.* XX, 199. Cf. Ps. Sol. iv. 2 f. where the typical Sadducee is described as 'severe of speech in condemning offenders in judgement; and his hand is among the first upon him (in execution of sentence) as (if moved only) by devotion (to God)'. See also Billerbeck, *Kommentar*, II, 819; IV, 349 f.

These considerations suggest that it is probably a mistake to look about for some historical person who may have laid down the Sadducean programme or embodied the Sadducean ideal;[1] for there is no such ideal or programme. The Sadducees of history are a body of practical men running the affairs of their nation on what would nowadays be called common-sense lines, making the best bargain they can for their people—and incidentally for themselves—in the existing circumstances. For ideals and programmes we must look elsewhere, to the men who wrote the Apocalypses, codified the Law and the Tradition, or founded the community of the Essenes.

That being so we ought to look for the origin of the party name in the sphere in which the Sadducees lived and worked—international politics. And in this sphere we come upon what is at least a possible explanation.

In the bilingual tariff inscription of Palmyra[2] dated A.D. 137 we find an Aramaic word *SDḲY'* corresponding to the Greek word ΣΥΝΔΙΚΟΥΣ and describing a group of civic officials. These officers, who are mentioned along with others, are made responsible for the enforcement of the fiscal decree. It seems to me that we have here a likely explanation of the name Sadducee. We can trace the existence of σύνδικοι back to the fourth century B.C. in Athenian history; and we find them mentioned in documents of the Roman and Byzantine periods. In general, their task in Roman times seems to be threefold: (a) to give legal advice to the governing body of the community; (b) to represent the community in dealings with the Roman authorities; and (c) to look after the fiscal

---

[1] The theory that the party got their name from another Ṣadoḳ, who lived in the Greek period and either founded the sect or was an outstanding member of it, has no real support save in a Rabbinic account of Sadducean and Boethosian origins. This account may safely be dismissed as legendary; and the theory, even though it is backed by the great authority of Eduard Meyer, must be deemed to explain *ignotum per ignotius*.

[2] *C.I.S.* Aram. 3913 (pt. II, vol. III, fasc. I (1926), pp. 33–73). The inscription is given, with commentary, by G. A. Cooke, *N.S.I.* no. 147.

interests of the community. It can, I think, be shown that this is a fair description of the functions performed by the Sadducees in the Jewish community; and I believe that the history of the Sadducees, or Syndics of the Jews, was something like this.

The Sadducees were originally the body of leading men in the Jewish nation, who under the leadership of the Hasmoneans formed an executive, administrative, and judicial council. This council was at first known as the γερουσία or senate: the name is used in Judith and the first three books of Maccabees. On Jewish coins it is called *ḥeber hayĕhudîm*; and later we find the name *Sanhedrin*. This last is the transliteration of the Greek συνέδριον; and it is not unlikely that *ḥeber* is a translation of the same Greek word.[1] One of the names for a member of this council was σύνδικος or Syndic, and the name Sadducee was the result of transliterating the Greek word into Aramaic or Hebrew. The Sadducees themselves did not connect the name with the high priest Zadok: they preferred another and more flattering false etymology which derived the name from the root *ṢDḲ* meaning righteous.[2]

We turn now to the Pharisees; and it is natural to begin with the opposition between the Pharisees and Sadducees. The differences between the two parties are recorded in Josephus and in the Rabbinical literature: we can also obtain information on some points from the New Testament. The material is collected by Schürer[3] and Billerbeck,[4] and it has recently been carefully discussed by Finkelstein[5] and Lauterbach.[6] In the light of their treatment it is probably a mistake to describe any of the matters in dispute between Pharisees and Sadducees

[1] See Wellhausen, *Phar. u. Sadd.* p. 41.
[2] See my *Sayings of Jesus*, pp. 295 f., and cf. *Enoch*, CII, 10 (ed. C. Bonner, p. 63); *Assumption of Moses*, VII, 3; Ephraim, *Evangelii Concordantis Expositio*, ed. Aucher and Moesinger, p. 288.
[3] *G.J.V.*[4], II, 449 ff. [4] *Kommentar*, IV, 344 ff.
[5] *Harvard Theological Review*, XXII (1929), 185–261; *The Pharisees* (1938).
[6] *Hebrew Union College Annual*, VI (1929), 69–139.

as unimportant. But there are issues that emerge as having been generally felt to be of critical moment. They are marked by the fact that in each case the Pharisees put forward a positive doctrine which the Sadducees simply reject.

(i)

The Pharisees believe in a divine purpose in history. The whole course of events is overruled by divine providence in accordance with a divine purpose. (Josephus translates this doctrine for his Gentile readers into terms reminiscent of the Stoic philosophy.) The Sadducees deny this and insist strongly on the freedom of the individual to shape his own life, and, to that extent, the course of history.

(ii)

The Pharisees believe in a future life where men are rewarded or punished according to their behaviour in this.[1] The Sadducees hold fast to the old doctrine of Sheol and reject this innovation.[2]

(iii)

The Pharisees have a developed angelology and demonology, which the Sadducees reject.[3]

---

[1] In Josephus this doctrine becomes—again for the benefit of Gentile readers—the immortality of the soul and its reincarnation in another body. But behind the sophisticated terminology the Pharisaic doctrine of the resurrection is plain enough.

[2] In this the Sadducees hold fast to Scripture and reject tradition. For Sheol is the doctrine of the Old Testament. In holding fast to the 'Biblical' doctrine the Sadducees show themselves true Semites. Cf. Wellhausen, *Reste Arabischen Heidentumes*, pp. 163 f. We may recall the derision with which Mohammed's teaching about resurrection and judgement was received by the Arabs in the early stages of his prophetic career. Cf. Muir, *Life of Mohammad* (1923), pp. 78, 97. The Sadducean belief in Sheol is transformed, and in some measure misrepresented, by Josephus (*B.J.* II, 165; *Ant.* XVIII, 16).

[3] Acts xxiii. 8. This is the only *testimonium* for this article of Sadducean disbelief. Cf. Moore, *Judaism*, I, 68; Meyer, *op. cit.* II, 297; Finkelstein, *The Pharisees*, I, 160–85. It is unlikely that the Sadducees denied outright the existence of angels and demons; for such beings are mentioned in Scripture. What they rejected was the developed doctrine of the two kingdoms with their hierarchies of good and evil spirits.

(iv)

The Pharisees recognise as the supreme authority in religion the Scripture plus Tradition. The Sadducees recognise Scripture only.

The last of the four points is not directly important for our purpose. It is sufficient to say that it gives the fundamental position taken by the Sadducees in rejecting the characteristic teaching of the Pharisees: sound Biblical doctrine and no beliefs for which there is not clear warrant in Holy Writ.

With regard to the other three points we must go further. The second and third are best disposed of in the careful words of G. F. Moore.[1] 'The eschatology of Judaism has an unmistakable affinity to that of the Zoroastrian religion in the separation of the souls of righteous and wicked at death, and their happy or miserable lot between death and the resurrection, and in the doctrine of a general resurrection and the last judgement with its issues. The resemblances are so striking that many scholars are convinced that this whole system of ideas was appropriated by the Jews from the Zoroastrians, as well as that Jewish angelology and demonology were developed under Babylonian and Persian influence.'

The first point, providence and free will, demands a closer examination. And it is important to see clearly what it is that the Sadducees are concerned to deny. Josephus says:[2] 'The Sadducees, the second of the orders, do away with Fate altogether, and remove God beyond, not merely the commission, but the very sight (ἐφορᾶν) of evil. They maintain that man has the free choice of good or evil, and that it rests with each man's will whether he follows the one or the other.'

---

[1] *Judaism*, II, 394.
[2] *B.J.* II, 164 f. (Thackeray's translation).

It does not seem to me that the Sadducees are here attempting to deny Providence altogether and to remove God from all contact with the world after the manner of Epicureanism. It is the problem of evil with which they are concerned. They would allow that God is the cause of the good things that happen in the world. They could do no other, for Scripture asserted it plainly enough. What they would not allow was that God was in any sense the cause of evil, either by direct action or by toleration. They maintained that good and evil are matters of free human choice and, we may suppose, that man in choosing chooses the consequences that will follow from his decision. In other words the Sadducees, in dealing with the problem of evil, are still maintaining the positions adopted by Job's comforters.[1] At the same time they are rejecting another solution of the problem which explained evil by means of the demons and their prince. It was involved in this explanation that God had either created these evil forces or, at least, tolerated their existence; and this meant that the theology based on the explanation was dualistic, even if the dualism was qualified by the fact that the toleration of evil was only for the time being. But here again we cannot but notice the resemblances between the doctrine rejected by the Sadducees and the doctrines of Zoroastrianism.

The result is that with regard to the most characteristic doctrines of the Pharisees the captious Sadducean critic could say with no little plausibility: 'This is not the religion of Israel as set forth in our Scriptures; it is the religion of Persia.' And that, I suggest, is what they did say. The word Pharisee originally meant simply 'Persian'; and it was applied to the innovators in theology in much the same way that the term 'Romaniser' has been used in theological controversy in our own day. The name stuck, and at a later date was furnished with an edifying etymology. It was explained that it was

[1] And Ben Sira, Ecclus. xv. 11–20; xxi. 27, 28.

really connected with a Hebrew root meaning 'to separate', and so signified that those who bore it were separated from all that is abominable[1] in God's sight.

To sum up. The Sadducees appear more definitely than ever as a political order. Their influence on the development of the Jewish faith is seen to be negligible. In theology they are the representatives of an ossified orthodoxy with no guiding principle except *quod semper, quod ubique, quod ab omnibus.* Consequently, when the Jewish state ceased to exist as a political entity, and the Temple, the centre of the traditional ritual, was destroyed, the Sadducees simply faded out of the picture.

The living branch of Judaism was the Pharisaic. The Pharisees were doubtless orthodox in the sense of holding to the old ways and the central doctrines of the religion of Israel; but they were also receptive to new ideas. I am not concerned to decide the question whether their characteristic doctrines were derived from Persia or were the development—under Persian influence—of ideas already implicit in Hebrew religion. The point is that the new ideas were developed, and developed by the Pharisees. They were the upholders of 'tradition'; but the tradition of the Pharisees was a living, growing thing,[2] and the future of Judaism as a religion lay with them.[3] And finally their characteristic doctrines—the

---

[1] It should be noted that the meaning 'Separatists' was supplied by the Pharisees themselves, and *sensu bono.* This meaning was, I think, already recognised in Pharisee circles by the middle of the first century A.D. and is played upon by St Paul in Gal. ii. 12 (see my *Teaching of Jesus,* 241 f.). It appears in Christian literature in Ps.-Tertullian, *Adv. omn. haer.* 1 (a work in its present form perhaps to be attributed to Victorinus of Pettau (*ob.* 304); see Altaner, *Patrologie²,* p. 152). Here it is explained that the Pharisees got their name through being separated from the rest of the Jews through their additions to the Law.

[2] 'On leur fait tort quand on les représente comme retardataires; certes ils le sont au prix du christianisme, mais à l'intérieur du judaïsme, en regard des Sadducéens, ils incarnent le progrès' (H. Duesberg, *Le Roi Hérode,* p. 202).

[3] When we meet them in the Gospels, they have become by far the most influential minority in Israel. It is evident from the testimony of the Rabbinical

doctrines which, on my view, earned them their nickname—
became the background for the earliest Christian theology.

There is, however, another aspect of Pharisaic beliefs and
hopes which is important for our purposes: they cherished
very definite ideas about the realisation of the Israelite ideal
at a time not too remote from their own day and within the
borders of their own land. In this matter we are not dependent
on the second-hand testimony. We have their own account in
the so-called Psalms of Solomon, a collection of eighteen
poetical pieces which can be dated with almost complete
certainty about the middle of the first century B.C. Moreover,
we have them in a Greek version, that is, at only one remove
from the original. And there can be very little doubt that
the collection is of Pharisaic origin. There is a further point
which, I think, requires special emphasis: the collection—un-
like most of the extant literature of the kind—appears to have
been put together for some kind of liturgical purpose. Where
was it to be used? It is not possible that these violently anti-
Sadducean songs can have been meant for the service of the
Temple. Were they composed for the Synagogue? Or for
the fellowship gatherings which appear to have played so
large a part in Pharisaism? We cannot tell. The one thing that
is clear is that the Psalms of Solomon do not look like a set of
quiet meditations of the individual: they suggest a community
singing or chanting. They are nearer to propaganda than to
private devotions.[1]

literature that Pharisaism was strong enough, not only to impress the masses,
but also to attract numbers of individuals whose performance, for one reason
or another, did not tally with its ideals. Such people are not peculiar to
Pharisaism. They appear wherever lofty ideals are set up in face of human
frailty, or where the prestige of a movement makes it worth while for the
worldly-minded to attach themselves to it. And the Rabbinic protests against
bogus Pharisees, from the time of R. Joshua b. Hananiah (c. A.D. 90) onwards,
have their parallels in the Cynic protests against the sham Cynics of the second
century A.D., and the solemn warnings of Christian preachers, throughout
the history of the Church, to unworthy bearers of the Name.

[1] To call Ps. Sol. xvii the Marseillaise of the kingdom of God, would,
I think, be to go much too far—in the right direction.

The fact that the Psalter of Solomon seems to be meant for the use of a community serves to remind us of the fact, now increasingly recognised by scholars, that the Pharisees were organised in communities, with definite rules and officers, regular times of meeting (usually on the eve of the Sabbath), and proper forms of procedure for the probation and admission of new members. These communities appear to have drawn the bulk of their members from the middle strata of urban society. The average Pharisee comes from the shop-keepers and skilled artisans. The leaders of the communities are often men with Rabbinical learning (Scribes); but the majority of the Pharisees were not scholars, nor were all the scholars Pharisees (the Sadducees appear to have had their scholars, though it is probable that the majority of the Scribes were also Pharisees).

The fact that the Pharisees were organised in this way probably explains the great influence they were able to exert in the New Testament period. Though small in numbers they were a compact and disciplined body capable of united and decisive action. Moreover they were together. The great majority of them appear to have been concentrated in Jerusalem itself: so that when a Gamaliel expressed an opinion in the Sanhedrin, everyone knew that there in the capital he had behind him 4000 or 5000 men of firm conviction and iron determination, apart altogether from adherents and sympathisers. In these circumstances it is not surprising to learn that the Sadducees had to bow, however unwillingly, to the findings of Pharisee Scribes, and that even in matters of Temple ritual.

The existence of this solid phalanx of convinced and determined men was not merely a feature of the Jewish religion of the time: it was a factor of the highest importance in the social and political life of Palestine. It was so when the dying Alexander Jannaeus advised his wife to come to terms with the Pharisees: it was so in the days of Herod the Great who spared few and trusted none, but who deemed it wise not to antagonise the Pharisees: it was still so during the Ministry of Jesus and in the days of the Primitive Church.

A remarkable confirmation of all this is furnished by a passage in Josephus,[1] where, instead of philosophising about the Pharisees, he gives us the plain words of his source. In this case the source seems to be Nicholas of Damascus, the friend and court-historian of Herod the Great. It is interesting to see how the Pharisees appeared to an outsider whose sympathies were with the government. To him they are a doctrinaire and opinionated sect, hostile to the government and always ready for intrigue, sabotage or armed rebellion. No doubt this report is biased and must be treated with reserve, but it cannot be simply dismissed. On the contrary there is a considerable element of truth in it, to which the Psalms of Solomon, the *Benedictus* and *Magnificat* all bear witness.[2]

We thus get a picture of the three parties in Judaism in the time of Christ: the Essenes despairing of this world and indifferent to politics, withdrawn into themselves and occupied with the 'religious' life; the Sadducees on the whole content with the *status quo*, with the old-time religion, and bending all their efforts to make the existing order last out their time; the Pharisees with their firm faith in the purpose of God in history, a purpose intimately bound up with the destiny of Israel and Israelites, looking always for the day when God would sweep away existing evils and establish in a place worthy of Israel an Israel worthy of that place.

And it is the Pharisees who have the ear of the people. The nature of the ends to be realised determines the main outlines of the Messianic picture, in so far as the Messiah is brought in

---

[1] *Ant.* XVII, 2, 4, § 42.
[2] Note that in Mark xii. 13–17 the question of the Pharisees and Herodians has to do with politics and patriotism rather than with the technicalities of the Torah.

as a necessary agent for the fulfilment of God's plan and the establishment of God's kingdom. And here again, if we ask how the average godly and patriotic Jew of our period imagined the Lord's Anointed, I do not think we can have a better picture than that given in the Psalms of Solomon.[1]

There are four passages in the collection, which are specially relevant to our inquiry: viii. 27–30, xi, xvii and xviii. Of these the most instructive are Pss. viii and xvii, for they give the leading ideas of the collection in the simplest and clearest form: corruption within Israel, punishment of Israel by God at the hands of the Gentiles, restoration of Israel by God at the hand of his Anointed. These are perennial themes; in the Psalms of Solomon the first two have their special exemplification in the misconduct of the later Hasmonean priest-kings and the destruction of the national independence by Pompey. The writer returns again and again to describe the wickedness of the Sadducean Jewish aristocracy and the blasphemous presumption of the Roman invader; but his last word is of deliverance to come, his most earnest prayer that it may come quickly.

O God, send thy mercy upon us and pity us;
Gather together the dispersed of Israel with mercy and kindness...
O our God, do not disdain to notice us,
Lest the Gentiles swallow us up as if there were no deliverer.

(viii. 27 f., 30)

[1] Again it may be urged that the Psalms of Solomon give a very inadequate picture, which must be supplemented from other documents (e.g. Similitudes of Enoch). Perhaps. But it must be remembered that the bulk of the hearers of Jesus were simple people. It is extremely unlikely that they possessed all the texts in Charles's *Apocrypha and Pseudepigrapha* (or even all that were in existence at the time); and it is certain that they did *not* have Charles's commentaries. Consequently the views of the average man may well have been less refined than those of twentieth-century experts on the subject. But it was the common people who were under the influence of the Pharisees, who repented on the preaching of John, who were 'ready to do anything on his advice', who enjoyed listening to Jesus, who cheered him into Jerusalem, and in the end preferred Barabbas. In all this I think they were consistent with themselves and with our most reliable evidence about the nature of the Messianic hope.

The meaning of 'deliverer' here is made clear by verse 11 where the Hasmonean priest-kings are described as plundering the holy things as if there were no 'inheritor-deliverer'. The Hasmoneans in assuming the royal dignity were taking the place of the rightful heir of the Davidic dynasty, destined by God to deliver Israel. This Davidic King-Messiah is the agent of national redemption, and, what is more, the only legitimate agent.

It is to be noted that the restoration of the dispersed of Israel to their own land is a principal element in the description of the coming deliverance. It is the theme of Ps. Sol. xi, and it appears in xvii. 31 and 44. It is already present in Isa. lxvi. 18 ff., in Ben Sira's picture of the happy future (Ecclus. xxxvi. 10), and in the hymn of thanksgiving which follows Ecclus. li. 12 in the Hebrew; and it recurs in Baruch iv, 36–v. 9 and in Philo's sketch of the Messianic hope (below, pp. 32 f.). Probably we should add the Mishnah, *Eduy.* viii. 7, which may readily be interpreted in this sense. *Ass. Mos.* x, like *Eduy.*, assigns the restoration of the Dispersion to Elijah. (See *J.T.S.* XLVI (1945), 42–5, and below, pp. 30 ff.)

The fullest description of the coming Messianic deliverance is given in Ps. Sol. xvii. It begins with the assertion of the sole sovereignty of God and a confession of Israel's faith in him alone. The Psalmist then goes on to say that, under God and by God's appointment, there is a single legitimate royal dynasty in Israel—the house of David. But the monarchy has been usurped by another line—the Hasmonean. God has overthrown these upstarts by the hand of the Roman Pompey whose momentary triumph must be regarded as the just judgement of God on the unrighteousness rampant in Israel. At the same time the Gentile instrument of the wrath of God, just because he was a Gentile and ignorant of the true religion, 'behaved arrogantly and his heart was alien from our God' (verse 13). His fate is described elsewhere (ii. 26–30). But the punishment of Israel's sins, the overthrow of the

Hasmonean usurpers, and the miserable end of the Roman oppressor, cannot be the last word. These things are but the preliminaries to the unfolding of God's purpose of good for Israel. This purpose is to be achieved, under God, by the rightful redeemer, the Davidic King-Messiah, whose accession to the throne of his fathers is now eagerly expected.

Behold, O Lord, and raise up for them their king, the son of David
Against the time which thou, O God, choosest, for him to begin
    his reign over Israel thy servant,
And gird him with strength to shatter unrighteous rulers,
And to purge Jerusalem from Gentiles that trample her down to
    destruction;
By (his) wisdom and (his) righteousness to expel sinners from the
    inheritance;
To destroy the pride of the sinner as a potter's vessel;
With a rod of iron to break in pieces all their resources;
To destroy the lawless Gentiles with the word of his mouth,
So that, at his threatening, Gentiles shall flee before him;
And to convict sinners for the thoughts of their heart.

And he will gather a holy people whom he will lead in righteousness,
And he will govern the tribes of a people sanctified by the Lord
    his God,
And he will not let injustice lodge among them any more,
Nor shall any wicked-minded man dwell with them.
For he will know them that they are all sons of their God,
And he will distribute them by their tribes on the land.
And the alien immigrant shall not dwell with them any more;
He will govern peoples and nations in the wisdom of his righteous-
    ness.

And he will have the Gentile nations to serve him under his yoke
And he will glorify Jerusalem with sanctification such as (it had)
    of old,
So that the Gentiles will come from the world's end to see his glory,
Bearing as gifts her sons that had fainted,[1]

[1] The people referred to here as having fainted are those who had lapsed—lost faith and hope in the divinely appointed destiny of Israel.

26

And to see the glory of the Lord with which he has glorified her
  and he will be a just and God-instructed king over them;
And there is no injustice among them in his days;
For all are holy and their king is the Lord's Messiah.

For he will not base his hopes on horse and rider and bow;
Nor will he amass for himself gold or silver for war;
Nor will he gather confidence from a multitude for the day of battle.
For the Lord himself is his king; his confidence and his strength
  are in his reliance upon God.

And the Gentiles will come before him in fear,
For he will smite the earth with the word of his mouth for ever.
He will bless the Lord's people with wisdom and gladness.
And he himself is pure from sin, that he may rule a great people,
Convict rulers, and extirpate sinners by the power of his word.
And he will not waver all his days (in his reliance) upon his God,
Because God has made him mighty by the Holy Spirit—
And wise by the counsel of understanding, with might and
  righteousness.

And the blessing of the Lord is with him in might, and he will
  not waver;
His hope is (set) upon the Lord, and who can prevail against him?
He is mighty in his deeds and strong in the fear of God,
Shepherding the flock of the Lord faithfully and righteously,
And he will let none among them faint in their pasture.
With equity he will lead them all
And there will be no arrogance among them that any among them
  should be oppressed.

This is the majesty of the king of Israel, whom God has chosen
To raise him up over the house of Israel to instruct them.
His words will be purified above the choicest precious gold;
In the assemblies he will judge the tribes of a sanctified people.
His words will be as the words of holy ones in the midst of
  sanctified peoples.

Happy are they that shall be born in those days,
To see the good fortune of Israel which God will bring to pass in
  the gathering together of the tribes.

God hasten his mercy upon Israel
To deliver us from the uncleanness of unhallowed enemies!
The Lord himself is our King for ever and ever.

The ideas expressed at length in Ps. Sol. xvii are epitomised in xviii. Here again we have the disasters of Jewish history construed as the divine chastisement of sins, and suffering as purification of Israel 'for the day of mercy in blessing, for the day of destiny when his Messiah is installed'[1] (xviii. 5).

The happiness of those destined to live under the righteous rule of the Messiah in the coming golden age is sketched in xviii. 6-9.

Happy are they that shall be born in those days,
To see the good fortune from the Lord which he will bring to pass
  for the generation to come,
Under the rod of discipline of the Lord's Messiah in the fear of his
  God,
In the spirit of wisdom and righteousness and might;
To direct men in works of righteousness by the fear of God,
To establish them all before the Lord
A good generation in the fear of God in the days of mercy.

The bright visions of the Pharisee Psalmist were not destined to be realised. Instead of the noble and righteous scion of the stock of David came the ambitious and ruthless half-caste Herod to control (under Rome) the destinies of Israel from 37 B.C. till his death in the spring of 4 B.C.

For the opinion of him held by those who cherished the Israelite ideal we may look at a little tract written some twenty years after his death, the *Assumption of Moses*, vi, 2-7.

And there will succeed them [the Hasmoneans] an insolent king, who will not be of the race of the priests, a man bold and shameless, and he will rule them [the Jews] as they shall deserve.

---

[1] The Greek text has ἀνάξει, which does not yield a tolerable sense. I conjecture ἀναδείξει. See E. Bikerman's article on the word in *Mélanges Émile Boisacq* (1937), pp. 117-24, and my note in *J.T.S.* XLVI (1945), 41 f.

And he will cut off their chief men with the sword and will destroy
(them) in secret places, so that no one may know where their
bodies are. He will slay the old and the young, and he will not
spare. Then the fear of him will be bitter unto them in their land.
And he will execute judgements on them, as the Egyptians
executed upon them, during thirty and four years; and he will
punish them. And he will beget children, who succeeding him
will rule for shorter periods.

After the death of Herod his domain was divided. Three
sons, who had eluded his murderous suspicions and contrived
to outlive him, shared in the distribution. Archelaus received
the greater part of Judaea, Idumaea, and Samaria with the title
of Ethnarch; Antipas had Galilee and Transjordania with the
title of Tetrarch; Philip, by all accounts the best of the three,
became Tetrarch of a district to the north-east of the Sea of
Galilee.

The material conditions in the country and the state of
mind of the people are strikingly revealed by the petition
addressed to Archelaus, who after his father's funeral had
made a declaration to the people in which he promised that,
when his status had been confirmed by the Emperor and he
took over the duties of sovereignty, 'it would be his earnest
and constant endeavour to treat them better than they had
been treated by his father' (Josephus, *B.J.* ii, 1, Thackeray's
translation).

Delighted at these professions the multitude at once proceeded
to test his intentions by making large demands. One party
clamoured for a reduction of the taxes, another for the abolition
of the duties, a third for the liberation of the prisoners.... Towards
evening, however, a large number of those who were bent on
revolution assembled...bewailing the fate of those whom Herod
had punished for cutting down the Golden Eagle from the gate of
the Temple.... These martyrs ought, they clamoured, to be
avenged by the punishment of Herod's favourites, and the first

step was the deposition of the high-priest whom he had appointed, as they had a right to select a man of greater piety and purer morals.[1]

This demand is threefold and covers the fields of economics, politics and religion. Relief from the grinding burden of taxation, abolition of Herod's gestapo methods in politics and release of the victims still in confinement, and a cleansing of the Temple and its personnel, these were the things called for. Archelaus soon made it plain that he was more than ready to play Rehoboam to his father's Solomon. He dealt drastically with the reformers and then left for Rome to lay his claim before the Emperor. He was followed by a deputation of his prospective subjects bent on exposing the enormities of Herodian rule to Augustus and petitioning for incorporation into the province of Syria.[2] Their requests were not granted and Judaea had to endure Archelaus until his misgovernment became unendurable to Rome and he was deposed in A.D. 6.

To this period belongs the short Apocalypse already referred to, the *Assumption of Moses*. Its composition should most probably be assigned to the years following the deposition of Archelaus. This work traces the history of Israel from the entry into the Promised Land to the reign of Herod and succession of his three sons (chs. ii–vi). This is followed (ch. vii) by what looks very like a description of the Sadducean administration of Judaea under the Procurators. Chs. viii and ix are more difficult. According to Charles[3] these chapters are out of place here: they are a description of the troubles that came upon Israel in the days of Antiochus Epiphanes, and their proper place is between v and vi. If this conjecture be not accepted, then chs. viii and ix must be

---

[1] *B.J.* II, 2 (Thackeray's translation).
[2] *B.J.* II, 84–92.
[3] *The Assumption of Moses*, 28 ff.; *A.P.O.T.* II, 420.

regarded as descriptive of the tribulations which are to precede
the great deliverance pictured in ch. x:

And then his (God's) kingdom will be manifest in all his creation;
And then the Devil will have an end,
And with him sorrow will be removed.
Then the messenger will be commissioned,
Who has been established in the highest place;
And he will immediately liberate them from their enemies.
For the Heavenly One will arise from his royal throne,
And come forth from his holy habitation,
With indignation and wrath for his sons.
And the earth will tremble: to its utmost bounds it will be shaken;
And the high mountains will be brought low and shaken;
And the forest will fall.
The sun will not give light and will turn to darkness.
The horns of the moon will be broken and she will be turned all to
    blood;
And the circle of the stars will be thrown into disorder.
And the sea will sink into the abyss;
And the water springs will fail,
And the rivers will be afraid.
For the Most High will arise, the Eternal God alone;
And he will come openly to take vengeance on the Gentiles,
And destroy all their idols.
Then happy wilt thou be, O Israel!
And thou wilt mount above the neck and wings of the eagle,
And...will be filled.
And God will exalt thee
And make thee to cleave to the heaven of the stars,
To the place of their habitation
And thou will look from the highest (place),
And wilt see thy enemies in the dust;
And wilt recognize them and rejoice,
And wilt give thanks and confess thy Creator.[1]

[1] For a discussion of the problems of translation and interpretation of this
passage see *J.T.S.* XLVI (1945), 42–5.

The main question of interpretation concerns the nature of the deliverance here described. Most commentators take the whole, or else the closing part, to be a description of the exaltation of Israel to eternal blessedness in heaven. In my opinion the closing sentences of the passage are not to be taken literally, but are simply the conventional figure for the possession of power and glory. (Cf. Isa. xiv. 13; Obad., iv; Jer. xlix. 16; li. 53; Ps. Sol. i. 5; Lk. x. 15; and the description of Israel as 'stars of heaven' in Dan. viii. 10; Enoch xlvi. 7.) The figure is very old. It appears in the so-called 'Poem of the Righteous Sufferer' *Tab.* II, ll. 46f. (Langdon, *Babylonian Wisdom*, p. 42): 'In prosperity they speak of ascending unto heaven. When they are in trouble they complain about descending to Irkalla.'

It is noteworthy that there is no Messiah: first comes the messenger and after him God himself and 'alone' (x. 7 *summus deus aeternus solus*). Lagrange points out (*Messianisme*, pp. 25 f.) that the Jewish war of A.D. 66–70 produced no 'Messiah' to lead the revolt against Rome. We may contrast the revolt of Bar Cochba in the thirties of the second century.

The picture presented by these apocalyptic writings is confirmed directly by Philo and indirectly by Josephus. The great bulk of Philo's literary output is concerned with the philosophical treatment of Jewish theology; but there are two places in his voluminous writings[1] where he allows himself to speak about the Jewish Messianic hope, and it is at once obvious that he shares the common expectation of a glorious future for Israel, the Messianic age. Its blessings are

(*a*) Security against attacks of wild beasts, which will become tame.[2]

(*b*) Cessation of war and hostility among men. So far as Israel is concerned, one of two things will happen. Either

[1] *De Praem. et Poen.* 15; *De Execr.* 9.
[2] On the wild beasts, see Pedersen, *Israel*, I–II, 325 f.; ibid. v, 22 f.; Ezek. xxxiv. 25, 28; Isa. xi. 6–9; lxv. 25.

(i) potential conquerors will retire from Israel's frontiers abashed by the moral superiority of Israel; or (ii) they will try an invasion and be decisively defeated, and that by the much smaller armies of the righteous. Some will be smitten by panic and fall an easy prey as they flee in disorder. All this is guaranteed by the oracle in Num. xxiv. 7 which is rendered by Philo thus: 'For a man will go forth, who leads to the field (of battle) and wages war, and will overcome great and populous nations, because God himself sends help to his holy ones.'[1] This leader will possess moral courage and physical strength of the highest order. Either alone would be sufficient to strike terror into his enemies, and both together will be irresistible. Those enemies who are unworthy to perish at the hands of the Israelites will be destroyed by swarms of wasps sent by God to fight on the side of the Saints (cf. Exod. xxiii. 28f.; Deut. vii. 20; Wisd. of Sol. xii. 8). Israel's victory will be followed by the submission of other nations, whether from love or fear or respect. For the saints will have three characteristics, majesty, severity, and beneficence, which produce respectively, respect, fear, and love. Where the three are all present together they will produce in subject peoples the inclination to yield willing obedience to their rulers.

(c) Material prosperity (proof text: Lev. xxvi. 4). This will be based on the abundant fruits of the earth provided by God.

(d) Long life and large families, with good health and complete physical fitness.

(e) Restoration of the Exiles to their homeland, or at least the reformed and converted ones among them. They will be released by their owners who will be ashamed to hold their betters as slaves.

Philo thus accepts the Jewish Messianic hope in its conventional form; and he does so because he finds it in the Bible.

---

[1] It will be noted that Philo does not even attempt to bring this Messianic leader into connection with his Logos doctrine. Cf. Loofs, *Dogmengeschichte*⁵, p. 46.

Josephus, on the other hand, is silent about it. For this attitude good reasons can be assigned. Josephus is writing after the disastrous end of the Jewish war of A.D. 66–70. We may surmise that his experiences in that campaign had done two things to him. They had completely disillusioned him concerning any realisation of the Messianic hope for Israel; and they had led him to the conclusion that the world-government which the Messianic hope promised to Israel had in fact fallen to Rome. He went so far as to reinterpret at least one Messianic prophecy in favour of the Emperor Vespasian.[1] What is abundantly clear is the nature of the glorious future that has eluded Israel and fallen to Rome.

The Mishnah is a step further along the road. The Messiah is mentioned only twice in the whole compilation (*Ber.* i. 5; *Sotah* ix. 15), and neither of these gives the normal picture. In *Ber.* the 'Days of the Messiah' seem to be distinguished from the present world. In *Sotah* the coming of the Messiah is not, apparently, to vindicate Israel, but to put an end to a state of universal corruption: though there *are* faint traces of a struggling Remnant who 'shun sin'. But the Messiah is a *deus ex machina*, a desperate remedy for a desperate disease.

Further confirmation of the nature of the Messianic expectation is afforded by the Synagogue liturgy. There the ideas and ideals of the Pharisees are reflected; and through the common worship these ideas worked their way into the texture of the average Jew's faith and hope. As an example we may take one of the most ancient elements in the liturgy, the *Amidah* or *Eighteen Benedictions*. I quote the fourteenth in the Palestinian recension. It is certainly pre-Christian.

[1] *B.J.* VI, 312 f. (trans. Thackeray): 'But what more than all else incited them to the war was an ambiguous oracle, likewise found in their sacred books, to the effect that at that time one from their country would become ruler of the world. This they understood to mean someone of their own race, and many of their wise men went astray in their interpretation of it. The oracle, however, in reality signified the sovereignty of Vespasian, who was proclaimed Emperor on Jewish soil.'

Be merciful, O Lord our God, in thy great mercy, towards
Israel thy people, and towards Jerusalem thy city, and towards Zion
the abiding-place of thy glory, and towards thy temple and thy
habitation, and towards the kingdom of the house of David, thy
righteous anointed one. Blessed art thou, O Lord God of David,
that buildest Jerusalem.

In this and other prayers the Israelite hope shines out clearly;
and if the convergent testimony of the Apocalyptic literature
and the Synagogue worship is not sufficient, we can add the
testimony of Jewish history in this period. For that history
shows that the Jews of Palestine were only too ready to
welcome any promising champion of the cause of Israel and
to take up arms in a holy war for the kingdom of God.

CHAPTER II

THE MESSIANIC HERALD

IT is of the essence of the matter that the Messiah is thought of as an irresistible, wise, and just ruler, who is 'mighty in his works and strong in the fear of God': and the central violent contradiction between the primitive Christian *kerygma* and the Jewish Messianic hope is that which sets the crucified Messiah of Christian experience over against the triumphant hero of Jewish fancy.[1] Now it is easy to see that the notion of a crucified Messiah is a stumbling-block to the Jews[2] (I Cor. i. 23): to complete the picture we have also to realise that the Jewish hope of a successful Messiah was equally a stumbling-block to Jesus.[3] It is from this point of view of the fundamental contradiction between the Jewish Messianic hope and Jesus's convictions concerning his own Ministry that the Gospel story becomes, in its main lines, an intelligible piece of history.

The Jewish expectation was then that the kingdom of God must triumph. In terms of history and experience that meant the vindication of all that is connoted by the word 'Israel'. The Messiah is the agent of this triumph of God: he comes

---

[1] A. S. Peake, *The Servant of Yahweh*, p. 214; cf. J. W. Bowman, *The Intention of Jesus*, p. 17.

[2] And to the disciples, of course, during the Ministry.

[3] Matt. xvi. 23, which may be freely, and I think correctly, rendered: He turned and said to Peter, 'Out of my way, Satan! You are a stumbling-block to me; for you are more concerned for a human empire than for the kingdom of God.' This last clause, which comes from Mark viii. 33 is well illustrated by the parallels in Esther viii. 12b (Rahlfs); I Macc. x. 20; and others from Josephus collected by Schlatter (*Der Evangelist Matthäus*, p. 518). The force of the rebuke is that Peter is ready to work and fight in the interests of an Israelite world-power after the fashion of the kingdom of David and Solomon: for the kingdom *of God* he does not really care at all. The tragedy of the situation lies in the fact that neither Peter nor any of the others believes that there is any real difference between the two things.

forth conquering and to conquer by divine power. And the immediate beneficiaries of this God-given Messianic victory are the people of Israel, the children of Abraham, the heirs of the promises made to the Fathers. It is all simple and straightforward. This comfortable faith was destined to receive two hard knocks: the first came from John the Baptist.

For our knowledge of the career of John we are dependent on two sources: the New Testament and the passage in Josephus (*Ant.* xviii, 5, 2, §§ 116–19).[1] The latter runs as follows:

> Some of the Jews, however, regarded the destruction of Herod's army as the work of God, who thus exacted very righteous retribution for John surnamed the Baptist. For Herod had slain John— a good man who bade the Jews to cultivate virtue by justice towards one another and piety towards God, and (so) to come to baptism: for immersion, he said, would only appear acceptable to God if practised, not as an expiation for specific offences, but for the purification of the body, when the soul had already been thoroughly cleansed by righteousness. Now when men flocked to him—for they were highly elated at listening to his words—Herod feared that the powerful influence which he exercised over men's minds might lead to some form of revolt, for they seemed ready to do anything on his advice. To forestall and kill him seemed far better than a belated repentance when plunged in the turmoil of an insurrection. And so, through Herod's suspicions, John was sent as a prisoner to the fortress of Machaerus and there put to death. The Jews therefore thought that the destruction of Herod's army was the penalty deliberately inflicted upon him by God to avenge John.

This fixes the lower limit for the death of John: for the defeat of Herod's army is placed by Josephus in the year A.D. 36. The death of John must have taken place before that date, how long before we cannot say with certainty. The upper

---

[1] The translation is that given by Thackeray, *Josephus the Man and the Historian*, pp. 131 f. In his opinion the authenticity of the passage is beyond question.

limit is given by Luke in the elaborate time-reference at the beginning of ch. iii of his Gospel. The data there supplied require a point between A.D. 26 and 34 for the beginning of John's ministry. The most precise of them—'the fifteenth year of Tiberius'—may give a more definite result. There has been much discussion about the correct interpretation of the phrase; but I think that the vital matters are settled by Fotheringham:[1] (i) that the reckoning of the regnal years of Tiberius begins after the death of Augustus, and (ii) that the regnal years are counted as beginning on the New Year's Days in use in different parts of the Empire. Accordingly, the fifteenth year of Tiberius may have been reckoned from the spring (1 Nisan) of A.D. 28 in Palestine, while in Antioch it did not begin till 1 September of that year. But in any case A.D. 28–9 marks the opening of John's prophetic ministry.

Luke (iii. 2) describes this event by saying that 'the word of God came upon John the son of Zacharias in the wilderness'. In other words, John received a prophetic 'call'. He found himself irresistibly caught up by the mighty current of the divine activity in human affairs, appointed to tasks which he dared not refuse, furnished with a message which he must at all costs deliver. He knew that God was 'making history' and that God would use him in the making of it. For John the religious life no longer meant the solemn ritual of the Temple, which was his hereditary vocation. Nor did it mean quiet meditation on the inherited treasures of Israel's devotional life, or mystical union with the Absolute. Rather it meant that he was apprehended by God the king, and that the divine authority and power entered into him and worked through him as he yielded himself to them.

This ministry has two distinctive features: it is a clear call to moral renewal and it has a clear reference to the Jewish Messianic hope. This is set out unmistakably in the Gospel

[1] *J.T.S.* xxxv (1934), 146–55.

account of John's preaching where the announcement of the approach of the New Age is put forward as the chief reason why there should be no delay in repenting of the past and bringing forth fruits worthy of repentance in the future. Even in Josephus the matter is only thinly disguised, by being overlaid with the Josephan veneer of Greek philosophy and Roman political ideas. John's call to repentance and amendment of life is tricked out in Stoic formulae and becomes virtue for its own sake. His eschatological sacrament becomes a kind of neo-Pythagorean ritual of bodily lustration, whereby inward and outward purity may match one another in due proportion. John's Messianic proclamation is reduced to a personal popularity that made him politically suspect: the voice crying in the wilderness is brought down to the level of soap-box oratory. But we need not complain. If we allow Josephus to speak in his own language, he confirms the Gospel account of John: in his own curious way he attests the call to repentance, the baptism, and the Messianic announcement, and—most important—the fact that the three things were intimately connected. John was not the first to preach repentance and moral reformation: he was not the first to make washing a ritual act charged with religious significance: he was not the first to indulge in Messianic propaganda. But he was the first to bring all three things together in an organic unity. With that 'threefold cord that is not easily broken' he drew the people after him and earned for himself the reputation of a dangerous agitator, who had better be put out of the way before he did some serious mischief.

It was this aspect of the matter that, according to Josephus, weighed strongly with Herod Antipas and led him to have John executed. And it certainly seems the most natural and likely explanation. In the Gospel, however, we are presented with a different story.[1] This account—significantly enough—

---

[1] Mark vi. 17–29; Matt. xiv. 3–12.

is appended to a paragraph (Mark vi. 14–16) in which we are told how the increasing popularity and influence of Jesus had attracted the unfavourable attention of Herod. The intention of the evangelist seems to be to draw a parallel between Jesus and John, and to indicate that Jesus at this point was in the same kind of danger that had formerly proved fatal to John. So far, he seems to be going on the same lines as Josephus. But he now goes on to tell a story in which the fate of John is the result, not of his popularity with the crowd, but of his outspoken comments on the domestic affairs of Antipas and Herodias.

Whence did Mark derive this account? There are indications which suggest very strongly—if they do not prove—that he had it from an Aramaic source, whether oral tradition or a written document; and it has been suggested that it may have come originally from the disciples of John, and so represent the *Passio Johannis*[1] as it was told in the Johannite sect. I am inclined to think that the story had often been retold, and had perhaps gained in the telling. As it now stands it has some features that are not easily credible. But there may be a solid substratum of fact. It may well be that John's denunciation of Herod's marriage with Herodias was the one thing needed to turn the Tetrarch's suspicion and fear into an active hatred that would not be satisfied with anything less than the death of the Prophet. It may well be, too, that Herodias felt that the only place where her marriage-certificate could safely be written was on the back of the death-warrant of John the Baptist. In that case both Josephus and Mark are in substance right, and they do not contradict but supplement one another.

Here we may pause to notice a rather curious fact. Both Josephus and the Gospels are agreed that it was Herod who was responsible for the death of John, yet there is no record

[1] J. Thomas, *Le Mouvement Baptiste*, pp. 110 f.

of any activity of John in Galilee, and we tend to think of John's main activity as having been in Judaea—*where Herod's writ did not run*. This idea that John worked in Judaea derives from Matt. iii. 1, 'the wilderness of Judaea', unsupported by the other two; for Mark (i. 4) locates him 'in the wilderness' simply, and Luke (iii. 3) adds that he came preaching all over the Jordan valley. Moreover, the Fourth Gospel (i. 28) places John's activities on the far side of the river. All this suggests very strongly that John's main centre was in Peraea; and this in its turn recalls to mind the fact that Herod Antipas was Tetrarch of Galilee *and Peraea*; and it also squares very well with the statement of Josephus that John was imprisoned and eventually put to death in the Peraean fortress of Machaerus near the Dead Sea.

In this connection it is perhaps significant, at any rate it is a matter for consideration, that Matthew tells us of two occasions on which Jesus took to flight (ἀνεχώρησεν— Matt. iv. 12; xiv. 13). One is on hearing of the arrest of John, the other on hearing of his death. In the first case he goes to Galilee; but leaving Nazareth he settles at Capernaum, which is admirably situated for a further move out of Herod's territory altogether. In the second case it is to an uninhabited spot on the shore of the Sea of Galilee; and shortly afterwards he does in fact cross Herod's frontier into the territories of Tyre and Sidon. If there is anything in this, it may signify that the connection between John and Jesus was a good deal closer than that between John and the majority of people who received his baptism, and that it was of such a sort that Jesus too was politically suspect, in other words that he had too much to say about the kingdom of God.

The preaching of John depends on accepting the Jewish hope as it stands and adding to it one more proposition: 'Think not to say in yourselves "we have Abraham as our father"'—or in Paul's words (Rom. ii. 28): 'He is not a Jew, which is one outwardly; neither is that circumcision, which is outward in the flesh.' Put the two things together, and there seems no escape from the conclusion that the coming of the kingdom, the vindication of all that is truly meant by the name 'Israel', must inevitably involve judgement on those who bear that name unworthily. The 'Coming One' is like a consuming fire; or he is about to fell the fruitless trees; or he is to separate the wheat from the chaff. The coming of the kingdom, the Messianic triumph, will mean that the time has come for judgement to begin at the house of God. It is no longer possible to say without further qualification: 'Blessed are they that shall be born in those days, to behold the blessing of Israel which God shall bring to pass in the gathering together of the tribes' (Ps. Sol. xvii. 50). On the contrary, the word may well be 'Offspring of vipers, who warned you to flee from the coming wrath?'

The practical outcome of this is a call to Israel to repent while there is yet time, and to seal their repentance by a baptism, which—like the proselytes' baptism—shall mark the end of their old way of life and a new beginning as Israelites.

It is important to be clear about what is happening in all this. John does not change anything in the Jewish expectation. All he does is to upset the belief that when the expectation is realised, it will be a good time for anyone who can claim his descent from Abraham. He declares that it will be a good time for those who have prepared themselves by repentance, and the bringing forth of fruits worthy of repentance, and for them alone. For all the others, Gentiles and Jews alike, it will be swift and ruthless judgement. The expectation is as it was before: only the incidence of the rewards and punishments has been readjusted.

John's Baptism. In discussing this question it is necessary to distinguish—and keep distinct—two problems. The first concerns origins: whence did John derive the ceremony of baptism? The second concerns significance: what purpose and meaning has the rite in the context of John's mission to Israel? To the former question the most varied answers are given. The rite is of Jewish origin and is modelled on the ritual washings prescribed in the Law. Or, in particular, it is an adaptation of the ritual immersion undergone by proselytes to Judaism. Or it is borrowed from the lustrations of the Essenes, or other baptist sects of the time, or, for that matter, from pagan ritual, Hellenistic or oriental. The fact that the rest of John's thought moves on orthodox Jewish lines, seems to me to forbid us to look outside Judaism for the origin of John's rite. There is no real evidence to connect John with Essenism[1] and none to link him with pagan religion.

If we confine the search to Judaism, the most likely of all the Jewish lustrations is the proselytes' immersion: and that for two chief reasons. First, the proselytes' immersion differs from the other Jewish washings in that it is a once-for-all rite that is not repeated: and in this respect it agrees with John's baptism, which equally seems to have been administered once only to each postulant. Secondly, the derivation of John's rite from the proselytes' immersion determines the kind of ideas to be associated with John's baptism: and those ideas fit admirably into the general picture of John's convictions and expectations.

But here we are faced by the objection that John's baptism cannot be derived from that of the proselytes; since the latter, it is said, does not appear to have become an established part of the ritual for the reception of proselytes until a date after the time of John the Baptist. This objection is stated very

[1] 'Some of those who have tried to reconstruct the life of Jesus have represented him as closely associated with the Essenes. That view is not only totally devoid of historical foundation, but it betrays a fundamental misconception of the meaning of his Ministry. If Jesus had joined the Essenes, he need never have been crucified' (C. H. Dodd, *History and Gospel*, p. 129). John the Baptist is even more remote from Essenism; and had he been an Essene it is most unlikely that he would ever have seen the inside of Machaerus.

fully by Joseph Thomas in his dissertation *Le Mouvement Baptiste*, pp. 61–88, 356–74; but I do not think that he proves his case. It still seems to me that the most natural interpretation of the Rabbinical evidence leads to the conclusion that the proselytes' baptism was a matter of discussion between the Schools of Hillel and Shammai, and that accordingly the thing itself must have been in existence before their time. That is, the practice of immersing proselytes may be pushed back to about the beginning of the Christian era.[1]

Now if the addition of baptism to the ritual for the admission of proselytes was a comparatively recent development at the time when John began his work, his adaptation of the rite to the purpose of his own mission becomes all the more pointed. For we know—Jesus himself bears caustic testimony to the fact—that the Judaism of the time had a vigorous and flourishing foreign missionary side to it. The Synagogues of the Dispersion all had their fringe of σεβόμενοι, *Metuentes*, God-fearers—pagans who were disillusioned about their ancestral faiths, were attracted by the pure monotheism and the lofty moral code of Judaism, and became what we should call 'adherents' of the Synagogue. Moreover, there was a regular, though smaller flow of full converts who definitely came over to Israel as full members of the community. These last were admitted by the threefold ritual of circumcision, baptism, and sacrifice.

It seems to me that the point—and it is a very sharp and stinging point—of John's procedure is that he deliberately invites the children of Abraham to submit to a rite which had been devised for the benefit of pagans. He says in effect: You call yourselves Jews, you claim to be the descendants of Abraham, you demand the privileges that belong to Israel. You have no right to the name, no right to the status; you

[1] See Billerbeck, *Kommentar*, I, 102–13; Moore, *Judaism*, I, 323–53; III, 107–14.

44

have forfeited all by your wickedness. You have only one chance. You must begin where the unclean Gentile begins—at the bottom. You must rediscover, and re-learn your Judaism from the beginning. Only so can you hope to have any part in the good time that is coming.

John's mission was not an end in itself. It is clear that he regarded it as the preliminary to something greater. His part was to prepare Israel to meet her God. The fundamental principles and motives of his work are thus incompatible with the idea of founding a new sect. John's business was not to found a new Judaism but to make better Jews: not to lay down a new code but get more faithful observance of the existing one. Hence it is significant that John's positive teaching (Luke iii. 10–14) does not amount to much. Many have found it something of an anticlimax after his preaching of repentance and his announcement of the coming Messiah. It is an anticlimax and it is important to realise why. It is because it is *Interimsethik*, the genuine article: telling men how to make the best of a bad job till the new day dawns. Strictly and logically John's converts should have gone quietly home strengthened by their experience at Jordan to live better lives, to be more faithful to the God of Israel, more obedient to the Torah, and to wait patiently for the fulfilment of the prophecies at the advent of the 'Coming One'.

But in fact the experience of conversion and baptism formed a link between John and his converts: they became his 'disciples', and the word implies the possession of a body of doctrine, and a system of discipline which bound them to their master and to each other.

There are traces of this discipline in the Gospels. It has two main features.

(i) *Common Prayer.* Luke tells us twice of this part of Johannite practice: v. 33, 'John's disciples fast frequently and say their prayers (regularly)'; xi. 1, 'Lord, teach us how to pray, as John taught his disciples'. In both places the information is given *en passant*: and there seems no good reason to doubt its truth. We know that the Rabbis gave specimen prayers to their disciples: and Luke tells us that the Lord's Prayer was Jesus's response to the request of his disciples. The natural interpretation would then be that John gave his followers a prayer or prayers for regular use by *all the members*. It is not merely that all pray but that all use the same prayers.

(ii) *Fasting*. Mark ii. 18 mentions fasting as practised by John's disciples. In this they resemble their master whose mode of life as described in Mark i. 6 is one of extreme simplicity and even austerity. That the description in Mark is correct is confirmed by the Q passage (Luke, vii. 24–35; Matt. xi. 7–19) which gives the testimony of Jesus to John. John was no wearer of soft raiment, no reed shaken by the wind. He came neither eating nor drinking. He was an ascetic. I am inclined to see in all this not so much the production of a set of 'spiritual exercises' as a revival of old Israelite ideals of the bareness and austerity of the desert life. The fruits worthy of repentance are to include this self-discipline in simplicity.

Lastly, what is the relation of Jesus to John's baptism? We know that the fact that Jesus submitted to it created great difficulties in the early Church. We can see them in Matt. iii. 14 f. and in the apocryphal Gospels of the Ebionites and Nazarenes. What need had a sinless Christ of John's baptism of repentance 'for the remission of sins'? The difficulty is a real one. It may, I think be faced, if we recall that the people who came to John had doubtless a great variety of motives. Some were burdened with a sense of their own sinfulness and futility. Some were drawn by the conviction that God was speaking once more to Israel by his servant the prophet and

wished to hear what the Lord would say to them. Some—
many perhaps—were driven by zeal for the greater glory of
Israel and Israel's God. It may be that Jesus saw in John's
activities the manifest working of God, and that he asked no
more than to 'fulfil all righteousness' by taking his place in
the new movement. I think it historically probable that our
Lord found in John's mission the starting-point for his own
work: I think it historically certain that he also found—the
record of the discovery is in the Temptation narrative—that
he must go far beyond anything that John had achieved or
even hoped for.

The task of John thus has two aspects. Negatively he had
to destroy the confidence that the Messianic hope was a gilt-
edged security from which every reasonably good Jew might
expect to draw a dividend. Positively—and it is here that the
real greatness of John lies—he set out to create a New Israel
to meet the coming Stronger One. He did not know—how
could he?— that it would need something thicker than Jordan
water to bind the New Israel together, that the New Covenant
that would create the New Israel must be sealed in Messianic
blood.

John is an impressive figure. A true prophet of the Amos
school. Stern in judgement, inexorable in his demands for
righteousness, breathing forth threatenings and slaughter
against all who do iniquity. No reed shaken by the wind—
there is no compromise, no give and take about him. No
wearer of soft garments—there is no trace of self-indulgence
in the grim old Puritan. Across the gulf of the centuries we
can still see clearly enough that austere and challenging figure,
and understand how he came to exert so powerful an influence
over his nation that even Herod feared him and thought it
safer to put him under lock and key. We know, too, that the
common people rated him at his true value. For them he was
a prophet.

Further, we know that his influence continued long after his death. His disciples were still to be found on the west coast of Asia Minor in the days when Paul was on his missionary journeys. We learn in Acts how Paul found half a dozen of them at Ephesus. Again Apollos of Alexandria was a disciple who had the baptism of John. It may also be that some of the Twelve were followers of John before they attached themselves to Jesus.

Further, in the life of the church there seem to be three practices which were taken over from John's discipline: baptism, fasting and common prayer.

In the Synoptic Gospels there is no record of Jesus or his disciples baptising. In the instructions given by Jesus to the Twelve there is no command to baptise. Yet in the earliest records of the church baptism of converts is a matter of course. The impression we get is that the rite is taken over from John's practice and made into a rite of initiation into the Church by being performed in the name of Christ.

Likewise, in the Synoptics we have a sharp contrast drawn between John and his disciples on the one hand as fasting, and Jesus and his followers on the other hand not fasting. Again, it seems not improbable that the custom of regular fasts in the Church may have been established by people who had learned it first from John.

Again in Luke we are told that the occasion of the giving of the Lord's Prayer was that the disciples of Jesus asked to be taught how to pray as the disciples of John were taught by their master. Jesus himself was accustomed to pray in solitude, and elsewhere he recommended the same practice to his followers. The Lord's Prayer is, from the point of view of the Lord's regular practice and teaching, an exception. But what a glorious exception!

Yet, when all is said and done, it is very little that we know about this prophet and more than prophet, who according to

Jesus was the greatest man who ever lived—outside the kingdom of God. We see enough to realise how great he was. And I think we can also see how lonely and tragic a figure he was. He was admired, respected, reverenced, feared—hardly, I think, loved. The least in the kingdom of God is greater than he. On the background of the Gospel we can see the magnificence of his failure. For his was the last supreme effort to make an unworkable system work. It was the last great attempt to carry out a wholesale religious and moral reformation within Judaism, to enforce the law of righteousness, to compel people to be good. In John's eyes this campaign of his was the last chance for the Jewish people. If they would not take it, they must look next for the judgement. In reality it was the last effort of the traditional Jewish legal religion to vindicate itself by producing changed lives. It failed, and where it had failed the gospel succeeded and took its place. In place of demands for righteousness fortified by threats of exemplary punishment, Jesus put the good news of the possibility of a real change of character and disposition wrought by faith and love. And because he knew the way to inspire in men and women that love and trust towards God which would transform human nature, he succeeded where John's threats of hell-fire had failed.

The story of John the Baptist is a tragedy, the record of a life of splendid courage, of single-minded devotion to great ideals. It is the story of a man who would not scale down the demands of righteousness to fit the opinions and practice of the time, who finally paid for his integrity with his life. The things he looked for did not come to pass, and the methods he used were not equal to the task. He belongs to the company of whom it is written that 'they received not the promise, God having provided some better thing concerning us, that apart from us they should not be made perfect'.

CHAPTER III

THE MESSIANIC MINISTRY:
PRINCIPLES

I T is at this point that the Ministry of Jesus begins, and the
second and shattering blow falls on the Jewish expectation,
in that the plan of salvation is challenged not in the details
of its application, but as a whole—both the end in view and
the means by which it is expected that the end will be realised.
This challenge as made is not simply a verbal criticism of the
Jewish theory. It is rather that the whole Ministry—the
teaching of Jesus, his acts, and finally the Cross, are a standing
denial of the current beliefs and hopes. This denial comes out
most clearly at three points in the story: the Temptation
narrative, the account of the events at Caesarea Philippi, and
the trial and death. In each case the Messianic reference is
clear and unmistakable. The Tempter says, 'If thou art the
son of God. . . .' Peter says, 'Thou art the Christ.' The High
Priest says, 'Art thou the Christ the son of the Blessed?' Pilate
asks, 'Art thou the King of the Jews?' The mocking ecclesiastics
by the cross say, 'Let the Messiah the King of Israel come down
now from the cross that we may see and believe.' Considered
from the point of view of the Jewish ideas of the kingdom and
the Messiah the Gospel narrative is a record of failure; but if
we see a little more deeply into the story itself it appears that
it is a failure to achieve something that was never attempted.
With these considerations by way of preface we may turn to
the evidence.

The starting-point is the two-document hypothesis; but we
are not spending any time on the Synoptic problem. We have
two typical documents Mark and Q: the one giving an account
of the Ministry and the other a summary of the Teaching. The

kernel of Mark is the Passion narrative which occupies a disproportionate amount of space, if Mark be considered as a chronicler of the Ministry; it is the portion of the record which most stubbornly refuses to disintegrate under analysis; and it focuses attention on the central fact—the Cross. In a sense it can be said that the whole of Mark's Gospel is really the Christian explanation of the bald statement of Tacitus concerning the Christians: 'Auctor nominis eius Christus Tiberio imperitante per procuratorem Pontium Pilatum supplicio affectus erat' (*Ann.* xv, 44). Q is essentially a record of teaching. Put the two documents together and you get the formula Passion Narrative + Teaching. And that formula agrees with what is given in the much-disputed *Testimonium Flavianum* (Josephus, *Ant.* xviii, 63 f.).[1]

Now about this time arises Jesus, a wise man, if indeed he should be called a man. For he was a doer of marvellous deeds, a teacher of men who receive the truth with pleasure; and he won over to himself many Jews and many also of the Greek (nation). He was the Christ. And when, on the indictment of the principal men among us, Pilate had sentenced him to the cross, those who had loved [or perhaps rather 'been content with'] him at the first did not cease; for he appeared to them on the third day alive again, the divine prophets having (fore)told these and ten thousand other wonderful things concerning him. And even now the tribe of Christians, named after him, is not extinct.

(Thackeray's translation.)

With a little more detail we have the same thing in the small collection of evidence which Klausner has extracted from the mass of Rabbinic material. The greater part of this

[1] That the passage is in substance genuine is made highly probable, if not certain, by the arguments of Thackeray (*Josephus, the Man and the Historian,* pp. 136–49) and Burkitt (*Theologisch Tijdschrift,* xlvii, 135–44). The chief difficulty in the way of regarding it as an interpolation is that of imagining what sort of Christian in the first three centuries could have thought it worth making.

polemical stuff is quite worthless for historical purposes; but Klausner did succeed in extracting a few points which can be put together to form a short narrative paragraph.[1] They may be summarised as follows: There are reliable statements to the effect that his name was Yeshu'a (Yeshu) of Nazareth; that he 'practised sorcery' (i.e. performed miracles, as was usual in those days) and beguiled and led Israel astray; that he mocked at the words of the wise; that he expounded Scripture in the same manner as the Pharisees; that he had five disciples; that he said that he was not come to take aught away from the Law or to add to it; that he was hanged (crucified) as a false teacher and beguiler on the eve of the Passover which happened on a Sabbath; and that his disciples healed the sick in his name.

Our two primitive types of document Mark and Q answer to the conditions of the primitive Church. The Passion story is the core of the primitive preaching in its missionary aspect— 'We preach Christ crucified'; 'I determined to know nothing among you save Jesus and him crucified'.[2] I should define Q as the earliest manual of instruction for the converted. Now the interesting thing is that the two-document hypothesis not only serves in the Synoptic problem; but the formula Passion Narrative + Teaching provides the ground plan of the most systematic of Paul's Epistles, that to the Romans. First comes. exposition of the Cross and then instruction in the duties of the Christian: the death of Christ for men and the new life of men in Christ. That is the Church attacking.

The Church on the defensive supplements this picture. In the fifties of the first century Paul can put the issue in a word: the Christian *kerygma*, the announcement of the Crucified

---

[1] J. Klausner, *Jesus of Nazareth*, p. 46.
[2] I Cor. i. 23; ii. 2; cf. Gal. iii. 1 'Galatians...before whose eyes Jesus Christ was placarded crucified.'

THE MESSIANIC MINISTRY: PRINCIPLES

Messiah is to the Jews a stumbling-block, to the Greeks foolishness. Why a stumbling-block? Because a crucified Messiah was a flat contradiction of Jewish hopes and convictions. Why foolishness? Because an executed criminal could not be saviour and benefactor. (Socrates was great in spite of his conviction and execution. It was a miscarriage of justice.) These considerations determine the main lines of defensive argument.

To the Jews it must be said that the death of Christ is the fulfilment of all the highest hopes of Israel. This line of argument is pressed most strongly in Matthew, with its constant appeal to Old Testament prophecies fulfilled in Jesus, who in this Gospel claims explicitly that he has come to fulfil the Law and the Prophets.

To the Gentiles it must be said that the Cross was a miscarriage of justice—and this is precisely the argument of St Luke. Jesus is one who goes about doing good; and the interest in the neglected and outcast has frequently been remarked as characteristic of this Gospel. In a word, Matthew and Luke are essentially apologetic works, the one addressed to Jews, the other to Gentiles. In the next century we find Justin's *Apologies* and his *Dialogue with Trypho* carrying on the double task.

The Christian case as presented to the world in the Apostolic Age is summarised in what is now known as the *kerygma*. This asserts: (*a*) that Jesus was descended from David; (*b*) that he fulfilled his Ministry among the Jews; (*c*) that he was crucified; (*d*) that he was raised from the dead and exalted to God's right hand; (*e*) that he will come again.

These assertions are enclosed in a framework which makes two further points: first that all that has happened is part and parcel of God's plan and was foretold by the prophets; and secondly, that the way of salvation is to recognise and submit to the will of God as it is now revealed in Christ.

53

The claims of the *kerygma* were supported by appeals to Old Testament texts, the so-called *Testimonia*, and by detailed accounts of the Ministry and the Passion. It is here that we are brought face to face with the main question concerning the gospels as historical documents. It is this. Were the stories told in the gospels created in order to provide fulfilment for the Messianic prophecies or were the prophecies sought out of the Old Testament in order to provide a *raison d'être* in the purposes of God for the particular incidents that went to make up the Ministry of Jesus? Has the evidence been faked to support the theory or has the theory been devised to suit the evidence? I have discussed these and allied questions else-where,[1] and here I must be content to say that, after every reasonable deduction has been made for human credulity, love of the marvellous, misunderstanding, propagandist zeal, dogmatic prejudices, and so on, there remains a solid and substantial body of historical material which makes an intelligible and credible story, a story which is consistent with itself and with the known conditions in the first century. The story is the story of the Ministry of Jesus. It is concerned with a period of not less than about eighteen months or more than about three years at the end of his life. Our main concern will be with two simple questions: What did he do? and Why did he do it? For the answer to the first question our main reliance will be on Mark; for the second on the collection of sayings of Jesus used in Matthew and Luke and commonly known as Q.

We begin with the second question: that is, we are to seek for the fundamental principles and convictions in the mind of Jesus, which gave form and direction to the activities that make up the Ministry. We shall take Q as our source and work on the basis that it is divisible into four main sections: Jesus and John the Baptist, or the Messianic hope; Jesus and

[1] *Bulletin of the John Rylands Library*, XXVII (1943), 323–7.

his disciples, or the Apostolic mission; Jesus and his opponents, or Torah and Tradition; Jesus and the Future, or Eschatology.[1]

(i) *The Messianic Hope.* For the understanding of Jesus's mind in the matter of the Jewish Messianic hope the starting-point must be the Temptation narrative as given in Q (Matt. iv. 1–11‖Luke iv. 1–13). The first question is whether it is genuine; and, in this connection, that can only mean: does the story go back to Jesus himself, and has it been transmitted to us substantially as he told it? It seems to me that the answer to the question is, Yes. Who in the Palestinian Christian community pictured in the first half of Acts could ever have invented the story? But if the story is something that Jesus told to his disciples—and I think that he probably did tell it to them in the days after Peter's confession, when they had come to regard him as the Messiah—then the important question is not whether it is an exact record of events that happened at precise times in places that could be indicated on a map of Judaea, but rather what Jesus meant to convey to his followers when he told them the story. We should regard it as spiritual experience of Jesus thrown into parabolic narrative form for the instruction of his disciples. That is to say, we must see in the three pictures that are set before us temptations which came to Jesus just because he had become aware of his own high vocation; and we must also assume that he deemed his experience relevant to the hopes and desires of his disciples. Otherwise why should he have told it to them?

It is not difficult to discover what the hopes of the disciples were. The evidence suggests that they were the hopes expressed in the Psalms of Solomon, the *Magnificat*, the

---

[1] For this reconstruction and division of Q see Major, Manson, and Wright, *The Mission and Message of Jesus* (1937), book II. This part has been republished separately under the title *The Sayings of Jesus* (1949).

Benedictus, and the preaching of John the Baptist. The reply of Peter to the first announcement of suffering and sacrifice as the essentials of the Messianic vocation (Mark viii. 31–3); the request of the sons of Zebedee, and its effect on the rest of the disciples (Mark x. 35–45); the naïve inquiry attributed to the Eleven (Acts i. 6); all point in the same direction. All go to show how firmly rooted in the heart of the average Jew was the kind of expectation that had found its classic utterance in Ps. Sol. xvii, and how incredible it was that the destiny of Israel and the Messiah should be anything but glorious triumph. To such men thinking in this fashion Jesus tells the story of his own temptations, in which he has discovered for certain that all the average Israelite's most cherished hopes are dupes, and his worst fears very far from being liars.

For a detailed exegesis of the text, reference may be made to *The Sayings of Jesus*, pp. 41–6. Here I must be content to state conclusions summarily. I think that the statement of F. C. Grant is in substance the right one:[1] 'One after another he [Jesus] rejects the ways proposed by political Messianism; the use of supernatural powers to provide earthly sustenance, the imperialist dreams of world-empire, the sudden, histrionic appearance of the celestial Messiah in the Temple Court.' Dr J. A. Findlay,[2] too, puts the matter well when he says that 'the Temptation-story...shows Jesus refusing to take the easy way of doing something *for* men instead of *with* them.' In other words, he refused to confuse his Messiahship with dictatorship. It may be put in this way, that what Jesus rejects in the Temptations are methods of 'bringing in' the kingdom of God: (*a*) the economic, with all that apparatus so well known to us in these days of 'five-year' plans and the like; (*b*) the game of political intrigue backed by military force;

---

[1] *The Economic Background of the Gospels*, p. 126.
[2] *Jesus and his Parables*, p. 142.

(c) propaganda which would eventually create an artificial nimbus for the national leader.[1] All three were familiar phenomena in the life of the time; the rumour of them had penetrated even into Galilee and Judaea (Mark x. 42). Augustus had been the most brilliant as he was the most conscientious exponent of the methods. Moreover, the result was one which we need not be in a hurry to depreciate. The Pax Romana, with its attendant benefits, was an achievement in which its author could, and did, take legitimate pride,[2] while his subjects expressed a boundless gratitude whose sincerity, notwithstanding the extravagance of the verbiage, we should not doubt. As we know, this gratitude and admiration issued eventually in the Imperial cult. In the Roman Empire at the beginning of the Christian era there were gods in plenty and no lack of potential faith and piety. The trouble was that there was not an occupant of the official Pantheon capable of arousing a real personal loyalty and devotion in the vast mixed multitude of peoples of the Empire. What Jupiter failed to do Augustus did—and Jesus; and the fierce struggle, which lasted till the beginning of the fourth century, between Caesar-worship and Christianity is the struggle between the cult of man-become-God and that of God-become-man, between a religion of apotheosis and one of incarnation. How clearly this issue was understood in the Early Church may be seen from Eph. iv. 8–10.

In the Temptations the Messiah is being invited to take the centre of the stage in one role or another. It is significant that each time the response of Jesus puts God in the centre of the stage; and each time the implication is made perfectly clear: even the Messiah is only God's servant—indeed, just because he is Messiah he must be pre-eminently God's servant. The Messiah is the chief man in Israel: then he must be the servant

---

[1] It was not for nothing that Antiochus IV was surnamed Epiphanes.
[2] See the *Res Gestae*.

of all. But above all he must be completely and unreservedly the servant of the Lord[1] (the *'Ebed Yahweh*).

But to begin thinking about the Servant of the Lord is to do the one thing that is fatal to Jewish Messianism. Jewish Messianism was extremely tenacious of life. Poverty, oppression, contempt and hatred could not kill it; it throve on defeats and disasters. Only to some better thing could it yield; and that better thing was found on the day when Jesus turned his back on the desires and hopes of his time to revive the half-forgotten ideals of the great prophet of the Exile.

We turn from the negative results of the Temptation story. Jesus has rejected the Jewish Messianic ideal even in the lofty form in which it is presented by John. What does he put in its place? After criticism, what constructive suggestions has he to offer? The answer to that question is given in the Q sermon (Luke vi. 20–49), commonly called the 'Sermon on the Plain'.

The structure of the passage is simple enough. It begins with Beatitudes and woes, which have the effect of separating the godly poor from the proud and haughty, the wealthy and self-indulgent, the worldly and godless. That is, we start from common ground shared with the Psalms of Solomon, the *Magnificat*, the *Benedictus*, and John the Baptist. For John, too, would have separated the sheep from the goats using much the same criteria. But immediately the sermon goes on to set this distinction on one side. The situation is approached from a fresh angle and the whole of the next section (vi. 27–36) is a demand for active merciful love towards the un-

---

[1] This idea has roots in the Old Testament: cf. Isa. x. 15; xxix. 16; Hab. i. 15 ff. S. A. Cook, *The Truth of the Bible*, p. 48, 'Consciousness of mission and destiny does not entitle men to forget that they are God's servants; and that it is God and not man who is behind the processes of history.' See also pp. 49 f. of the same work, and R. B. Y. Scott, *The Relevance of the Prophets*, p. 154.

lovely and unlovable. John says 'Offspring of vipers': Jesus
deliberately sets out to nourish the vipers in his bosom. And
all is based on the motive (v. 36), 'Be ye merciful as your
Father is merciful.' Here is a sharp contrast to the axe and
winnowing fan and devouring fire of John's expectations.
The wrath has given way to mercy.

But not only is the execution of judgement held up: the
judgement itself is withdrawn (verses 37–42). The Chosen
Few are not chosen to act as censors over the rest of mankind,
but for a career of service whose distinguishing marks shall be
a deep and sincere humility and a boundless generosity. It is
no longer the case that you must be just before you are
generous: rather it is now necessary to be lavishly generous
in order to be just. The Messiah of John's expectation would
be a strict and relentless judge: Jesus sees his vocation and it is
not so much to judge the faults of men as to heal their hurts,
to give them deliverance from the evil powers that hold them
captive.

And so (verses 43–6) even John's demand for fruits worthy
of repentance is transformed. It is not now a laborious striving
to maintain a certain standard of behaviour in view of a coming
judgement; rather it is a case of hearts that have been touched
by the tender mercy of God and producing spontaneously this
divine charity in their dealings with their fellows. The
Messianic office has been quietly transformed from the
administration of justice into a labour of love.

(ii) *The Apostolic Mission.* These simple and fundamental
principles determine the nature of the Mission Charge to the
disciples (Luke x. 2f., 8–16 ‖ Matt. ix. 37f.; x. 15f., 40; xi.
20–4). The Apostolic Mission must be an extension of the
Ministry of Jesus himself; and therefore it cannot be a proselytising campaign. For the business of proselytising is to win
adherents for a cause—to enlist recruits, let us say, for the
army of God; to enrol workers who will begin to build the

kingdom of God on earth;[1] to mobilise all the available man-
power in support of God's enterprises. But the Mission of
Jesus—and of his Apostles—is directed first of all to those
whom nobody wants, because they are no good to anybody.[2]
It is an offer of help to the foolish and helpless, not an appeal
for the support of the wise and strong. So the first apostles
are given as their message 'not a programme for human action,
but the proclamation of an act of God'.[3]

Yet there is a sense in which the mission of Jesus and his
disciples is an appeal to the people, an appeal for recognition
and acceptance. Some of the most tragic utterances of our
Lord are evoked by the refusal of the Jewish people to
recognise and accept him and the good things he offered.
'Jerusalem, Jerusalem, that kills the prophets and stones those
that are sent to her; how often I would have gathered your
children together, as a hen gathers her brood under her wings,
and you would not.'[4] 'And when he came in sight of the City,
he wept over it and said, "If only you had known, yes you, in
this your day, the things that would make for your peace!
As it is, they are hidden from your eyes."'[5]

(iii) *The Opposition.* The nature of this act of God can be
summed up in the historical fact that God's envoy earns the
title 'Friend of publicans and sinners', and by that very fact
finds himself at odds with the constituted authorities both
civil and religious. This is the secret of the merciless criticisms
to be found among the utterances of Jesus: Herod described

[1] 'Whenever the main stress is laid upon "building Jerusalem in England's
green and pleasant land", the Christian attitude to the world is abandoned'
(E. Bevan, *The Kingdom of God and History*, p. 56). Cf. C. H. Dodd, *History
and the Gospel*, p. 123.
[2] 'This is a standing characteristic of the Early Church and one that draws
down on the Church the contempt of the enlightened' (Celsus ap. Origen,
c. Cels. III, 44, trans. Gwatkin in *Early Church History*, I, 174). Cf. Lucian,
Peregrinus Proteus, §13: victimisation of Christians by clever rascals.
[3] C. H. Dodd, *loc. cit.*; cf. L. A. Weigle, *Jesus and the Educational Method*,
p. 116.
[4] Matt. xxiii. 37. ‖ Luke xiii. 34.   [5] Luke xix. 41.

as 'that fox', the Temple and its hierarchy as a 'den of robbers', the Scribes and Pharisees as 'hypocrites' and 'blasphemers against the Holy Spirit'. These hard sayings are Christ's judgement on the hostility of the authorities; and this hostility, in its turn, arises out of official concern at the activities of the Messianic Ministry. His friendship with the lower orders and his influence over them made him, like John before him, politically suspect to all those—Sadducees and Herodians— whose interest it was to maintain the existing order. At the same time, and for the same reason, he was theologically suspect to all those who saw in the scribal code and the Pharisaic practice the authentic Israelite ideal. So it came about that Jesus not only had to challenge the existing messianic dreams in the name of the kingdom of God, he had also to question the validity of Torah and tradition as the final expression of the will of God, and that in the name of his own Ministry, which for him *is* the rule of God.

I have discussed this matter elsewhere[1] and here must be content to quote my conclusions.

For Jesus the thing of first importance, the only thing of *any* importance is his own Ministry, that is to say his task of manifesting the perfect rule of God by being the Servant in perfect love of God and man. For him that is the only thing in the world that comes with an absolute and unqualified claim. Not even the Law can compare with this supreme obligation. That is not to say that Jesus rejected the Law or that he lightly disregarded any of its commands and prohibitions. It does mean that he did not hesitate to break through its restrictions in the interests of his own task, and that he reserved the right to criticise freely, not only the oral tradition and the scribal decisions, but even the written Torah itself.. . .

It is important to realise what this does not mean. Jesus does not claim to be a greater legislator than Moses, or a more learned lawyer than Hillel. He claims nothing for himself. He appears as

[1] *Religion and Law*, pp. 125–41, ed. E. I. Rosenthal.

the servant *par excellence* of the kingdom of God, and it is for the merciful redemptive work of the kingdom that he demands the fullest scope. If the Law stands in the way of that work, so much the worse for the Law.

(iv) *Eschatology*. As Jesus saw it the golden future for Israel did not lie in preserving the *status quo*; nor in a violent upheaval that would cast down the power of Rome and establish Jerusalem as the capital of a world-Empire; nor yet in the multiplying of converts (from without or within) to a Judaism of ever stricter orthodoxy and piety. The evidence of the Synoptic Gospels goes to show that he taught that all these ways must lead to disaster. This is clearly enough recognised in the 'political' sphere, where Herodians, Sadducees and 'Zealots' are concerned. It is implied also in the strictures on Pharisees and lawyers: the woes pronounced against them are not curses, but declarations that the way they have chosen is a road to ruin just as much as the ways chosen by the others. All are in the same boat. All the well-laid schemes, all the carefully planned programmes are doomed to frustration. There is no future for those delicate political manipulations by which the native princes and potentates and the representative of Imperial Rome maintain an uneasy balance of power (and a certain balance in the bank). There is no future for a fanatical nationalism that would seize the kingdom of God by force. And equally there is no fulfilment for those Utopian dreams which see the kingdom of God descending from heaven to confirm the correctness of scribal decisions and to reward Israel for obeying them.

The eschatology of Jesus, as it is given in the poem on the Day of the Son of man, differs from all these schemes in that, whereas they only propose a continuation of the present order in a more or less drastically modified form, it contains a real *eschaton*. It does not announce the latest development in the historical process but the last. Its finality does not consist in registering the most recent reading on the historical clock: it is the finality of the last word or the last judgement, a finality which makes time-measurement irrelevant.

Moreover, that finality has invaded the present moment. The Ministry *is* in a real sense the coming of the kingdom: the teaching *is* in a real sense the final word of God. By their response to these things men pass judgement on themselves. It is no accident that Jesus describes his own Ministry in similar terms to those in which he describes the Last Day.

You think I have come to give peace on the earth? No! On the contrary: division. From now on there will be five in one household, divided three against two and two against three. They will be divided, father against son and, son against father; mother against daughter and daughter against mother; mother-in-law against daughter-in-law and daughter-in-law against mother-in-law (Luke xii. 51–3 ‖ Matt. x. 34–6; Q).

If anyone comes to me and does not hate his father and mother and wife and children and brothers and sisters, yes, and his own life too, he cannot be my disciple (Luke xiv. 26 ‖ Matt. x. 37; Q).

I tell you, in that night there will be two in one bed, one will be taken and the other left; there will be two in the field, one will be taken and the other left; there will be two working the hand-mill together, one will be taken and the other left (Luke xvii. 34 f. ‖ Matt. xxiv. 40 f.; Q).

These sayings have to be set alongside those others which emphasise the coming of the kingdom in the beneficent aspects of the Ministry. When all are considered together, the meaning of 'Realised Eschatology' emerges with some clearness. First, there is the fact that the distinguishing quality of the *Eschaton* is not—if I may coin the word—postremity but finality. Secondly, this finality is twofold: the *Eschaton* is at once the supreme gift of God to men and the most unqualified claim upon them: it is the final revelation and the final judgement. Thirdly, these things are embodied in the figure of the Son of man. This symbolic figure, in the teaching of Jesus, combines the characteristics of the servant of Jehovah in Deutero-Isaiah and the Son of man in Daniel, that is to say, the supreme expression of the redemptive merciful love of God and the fullest assertion of the universal rule of God in the Old Testament. This figure of the Son of man is, at the same time, the delineation of the true ideal for Israel. Fourthly, the realisation of this ideal is intimately bound up with the Ministry of Jesus. That dream-figure the Son of man, who gives his life a ransom for many and comes in glory with the clouds of heaven, became historical reality on the day when Jesus of Nazareth, coming up out of the Jordan from John's baptism, took the first step on the road that led to Calvary.[1]

[1] Cf. W. Manson, *Jesus the Messiah*, pp. 155–8.

CHAPTER IV

THE MESSIANIC MINISTRY: PRACTICE

THE life and the teaching of Jesus illuminate one another, and the outline of the course of the Ministry, which follows, tends to confirm the interpretation of the teaching which I have already suggested.

The story, for all practical purposes, begins with the baptism of Jesus by John. Mark opens his account of the good news with John's mission, which probably commenced in A.D. 28/29. We do not know how long it had been in progress when Jesus was baptised. Nor do we know the length of the interval between the baptism and the beginning of the *Galilean* Ministry. Mark tells us that after John had been 'delivered up' Jesus came into Galilee preaching: he does not say that Jesus had done nothing to that point. Mark i. 14 gives a new point of departure; after John's arrest Jesus moved to Galilee. What is being dated is the inauguration of the *Galilean* Ministry, or, perhaps, the call of Peter (Mark i. 16–18). Peter's reminiscences may well have dated his call by reference to the arrest of John, just as Isaiah dated his by reference to the death of Uzziah. I have already urged that probably Jesus came to baptism under a strong sense of vocation.[1] This was more than confirmed by the experience which immediately followed the baptism. Jesus knew beyond a peradventure that he was chosen by God for a task greater even than John's. John's baptism, which was the climax of John's prophetic activity, was but the starting-point for the Ministry of Jesus. If we now go on to ask what differences, if any, can be discerned between the ways of John and those of

[1] See above, p. 47.

Jesus, the immediate and obvious answer is that given by
Jesus himself in the Q passage (Matt. xi. 18–19 ‖ Luke vii.
33–5). 'John practised strict austerity in food and drink; and
you said "He's a mad fellow": the Son of man practises no
such austerities; and you say, "Ha! a glutton and a tippler,
a friend of publicans and sinners."'

John was an ascetic; Jesus is not. That impression is
confirmed by the Marcan narrative on the subject of fasting
(Mark ii. 18–20). But this external feature points to a difference
that goes deeper still. It is not merely that Jesus eats where
John would fast. He eats with publicans and sinners and is
known as their friend (Matt. xi. 19 ‖ Luke vii. 34). In this
connection one story that is told by Mark is very instructive.[1]
It describes the call of Levi the publican, and then goes on to
tell of a meal at which Jesus created a scandal by eating with
the dregs of society, the publicans and sinners. The reply of
Jesus to the criticism passed on his behaviour was: 'It is not
the healthy people that need the doctor, but the sick. I did
not come to invite righteous people, but rather sinners.' In
Luke the meaning of the verb 'invite' is made more explicit
by the addition of the words 'to repentance'. I am convinced
that this edifying addition by Luke is a misinterpretation; and
that the original meaning of the verb in Mark is, as I have
translated it, to invite. If that is so, the most natural interpretation of the Marcan narrative is that which makes Jesus
the host of Levi and his friends.

On this, there are two things to be said. First, we may note
that the attitude of Jesus to these outcasts is in all essentials
that which he ascribes to the Father in the parable of the
Prodigal Son. That love of God which is so beautifully
portrayed in the parable is actualised in the events described
in the Marcan narrative. It is impossible to exaggerate the
closeness of the tie between the teaching of Jesus and his acts.

[1] Mark ii. 13–17 and parallels.

Secondly, there is the principle that a single story or saying may contain the whole Gospel in miniature.[1] What confronts us in these sayings and stories is not only the promulgation of the 'Law of Love', but also the demonstration of the Love of God in action.

Returning to the general question of fasting (Mark ii. 18–20) we may note another point which differentiates the Ministry of Jesus from the discipline of the Pharisees or the code of the followers of John. Asked why his followers do not fast he replies, not with a discussion of the value of fasting as a spiritual exercise, nor with a criticism of the fasts of hypocrites, but with the bald statement that a wedding feast is no time for fasting. Now to Jewish minds in the first century the wedding feast was a natural figure for joy, and in particular for the joy of the Good Time coming—the Messianic Age.[2] For the average Jew that meant the joy of the victory and the vindication of Israel. For Jesus joy is specially associated with the triumph of the redemptive love of God. There is joy in Heaven over the repentant sinner. At the return of the Prodigal the Father's house is filled with music and dancing. Jesus' rejection of the fasts is governed by the fact that the natural fruit of his Ministry is joy.

I make these points because they seem to me to illustrate a principle which, if well-founded, is all-important: that you may take up any single point in the Gospel history, and before you have been investigating it for very long, you will find the words and deeds of Jesus dovetailing into one another, and—what is more vital—the essential spirit and principles of the whole Ministry actualising themselves in the seemingly unimportant details of his teaching and his behaviour.

[1] I am glad to find that this view is shared by K. L. Schmidt, *Le Problème du Christianisme primitif*, p. 25. 'Chaque acte et chaque parole de Jésus contient *in nuce* ce Kerygma.'

[2] This means that this saying on fasting becomes a piece of evidence in favour of Realised Eschatology.

The sympathy of Jesus with the outcasts and failures of life—the actualisation of the merciful redemptive love of God—has as an immediate corollary the principle that the warfare of the kingdom of God is not against the moral down-and-outs—they, after all, are the victims of evil—but against those forces, without and within, that keep them down and out. That is the significance of the numerous encounters of Jesus with what are called demons and unclean spirits. Our instinctive dislike of these vestiges of primitive Semitic superstition should not blind us to the fact that Jesus saw clearly in the first century the thing that many of us in the twentieth still do not realise at all adequately: that the evil-doer may be, and often is, the victim of forces that seem to lie outside his own control altogether. Paul seized the essential point when he made the central task of Jesus consist in achieving the reconciliation of sinners and the condemnation of Sin.

The so-called 'Galilean' spring-time of the Ministry is the record of the first putting of all this into practice, with the immediate response of the spiritually poor and needy to the wealth of kindness that was being offered to them in God's name. But that fair light that shines on the early days of the Ministry in Galilee has its dark shadows. I have already suggested (above, p. 41) that the beginning of the work in the north may well be the result of a forced withdrawal from the southern districts of Peraea or Judaea or both, consequent on the arrest of John the Baptist. I think that we must allow more importance to the effects of John's activity on the early stages of the Ministry of Jesus than we commonly do.

However that may be, the Galilean period has some clearly marked results. First, and clearly outstanding, is the widespread reputation and the personal popularity of Jesus himself. He exercises an irresistible fascination over the multitudes. There is here something which may have a bearing on our interpretation of those stories which record the call of disciples.

For most of us the difficulty of the stories lies in the promptitude with which these men down tools and attach themselves to the itinerant preacher. But may this difficulty not be entirely imaginary? May it not be the case that here were dozens of men in the crowds that gathered round Jesus all eagerly waiting for a sign from him; and that the man who was chosen was looked upon not as a kind of martyr, but as a very fortunate person who had been granted an exceptional favour (let in on the ground floor)? This question is the more to the point if my ideas of the messianic hopes of the average Jew are anywhere near the mark. Secondly, and I think largely as a result of this personal popularity, Jesus becomes more and more suspect to the authorities. The people may have hazarded the guess that Jesus was John the Baptist risen from the dead:[1] certainly Herod Antipas might have felt justified in saying, 'This is John the Baptist all over again.' And from a purely political point of view nobody could blame Herod for holding such an opinion. After all, the pericope in Mark which describes the attitude of Herod follows hard on that narrating the mission of the Twelve; and while the Twelve were doubtless sent out by Jesus to extend his own work in his own spirit, it may not have appeared in that light to Herod, when he learned that propaganda agents were appearing in couples here and there in his territory making inflammatory speeches about something called the kingdom of God (the kingdom of Herod was good enough for Herod).

It is not too much to say that the Galilean Ministry had released forces which were becoming increasingly difficult to control. Jesus himself was being put into a dangerous position between the patriotic zeal of his followers and the suspicious fears of the Tetrarch.

The crisis comes, I think, with the so-called Feeding of the Five Thousand. At this point in Mark we are presented

[1] Mark vi. 14 reading ἔλεγον with BDW.

with two of the most extraordinary nature-miracles in the Synoptic tradition, the miraculous feeding and the walking on the water; and, on the whole, the ingenuity of scholars has been directed towards making these stories tolerable to modern minds by explaining them or explaining them away. For me the points of real interest and difficulty lie somewhat apart from the strictly miraculous elements.

The picture presented in Mark vi. 33–56 is one in which Jesus and his disciples set off by boat in an attempt to get away from the ever-present crowd. But the crowd refuses to be shaken off and follows the course of the boat round the shore of the lake. Before long Jesus gives up the attempt and comes ashore where the people are already awaiting him. The inference is that this meeting took place on the west side of the lake, and that the boat had not gone far when it was decided to land. Mark tells us that Jesus was sorry for the crowd because they were like sheep with no shepherd, which we tend to think means a congregation without a minister. But in Old Testament usage it regularly means an army without a general, a nation without a national leader.[1] Now Mark also tells us that the crowd numbered five thousand men; and the word he uses means men as distinct from women and children.[2] What Jesus saw on the shore of the lake was a maccabean host with no Judas Maccabaeus, a leaderless mob, a danger to themselves and everyone else. He speaks to them at some length and later they share a meal, at which Jesus uses symbols which afterwards came to be associated with the suffering and death of the Messiah. Then comes the

---

[1] For the metaphorical use of shepherd in the Old Testament see Num. xxvii. 17; I Kings xxii. 17; II Chron. xviii. 16; Judith xi. 19; Mic. v. 2–9; Nah. iii. 18; Zech. xi; xiii. 7; Isa. xl. 11; lxiii. 11; Jer. ii. 8; x. 21; xxiii. 1–8; xxv. 32–8; l. 6, 44; Ez. xxxiv; xxxvii. 24. It is primarily a royal or a Messianic title. The Messianic king is pictured as shepherd of Israel in Ps. Sol. xvii (above, p. 27).

[2] A fact which did not escape the notice of Matthew, who used it to increase the crowd and so enhance the miracle.

dismissal. First Jesus gets rid of the disciples, whom he sends off by boat. It is difficult to resist the impression that he thought that it would be easier to persuade the crowd to go home, if the disciples were not there; which suggests that perhaps the real sympathies of the disciples were with the hopes and wishes of the five thousand rather than with the purposes of Jesus.

What the crowd wanted we can readily guess; and the guess agrees with the plain statement of the Fourth Gospel that they wished to take him by force and make him king (John vi. 15). John further tells us that Jesus withdrew into the hills by himself, a point which is also made in the Synoptic narratives. It is clear, I think, that Jesus did not wish to be made a king; and this refusal in practice corresponds exactly with what we have already learned about his thoughts on Messiahship.

Shortly afterwards we find Jesus leaving Galilee and spending some time in the territory of Tyre and Sidon. I regard this withdrawal as a flight, but far more a flight from the dangerous enthusiasm of his friends than from the suspicions and fears of his enemies. The stay in Tyrian territory is followed in Mark's account by a visit to the Decapolis,[1] another district outside the frontiers of Galilee. The next notes of place are Bethsaida[2] and Caesarea Philippi[3] still outside of Galilee in the territory of Herod Philip.

It is here that we have the great turning point in the Ministry marked by Peter's recognition of Jesus as the expected Messiah. And here the clash between the two messianic ideals is manifest. What does Peter mean when he says, 'You are the Messiah'? And how does Jesus receive the statement? Mark's answer to the latter question is that Jesus forbade the disciples to speak to anyone about himself. The context requires us to add the words 'as Messiah'. As

---

[1] Mark vii. 31.   [2] Mark viii. 22.   [3] Mark viii. 27.

for the former question the answer is given almost immediately in Mark, when Peter indignantly repudiates the idea that the messianic destiny can be anything but glory and success. Jesus is equally uncompromising in maintaining that the task of the Son of man is of another kind and that its glory and success will be very different from the gaudy triumphs on which the hearts of Peter and the other disciples are set.

With that the calling of the disciples begins all over again.[1] The terms of discipleship are made terribly plain: he who swears fealty to me makes his compact with scorn and derision, defeat and death. From this point onwards three themes are closely linked in Mark's narrative: the relentless claims of Jesus on his disciples, the stubborn hopes and ambitions of the disciples themselves, and the repeated predictions[2] of the Passion of the Son of man.

At this point something must be said about the Son of man, for it is here in the Markan story that the Son of man becomes a figure of first-rate importance in the development of the Ministry. I have discussed the matter at length elsewhere,[3] and at this point I would merely summarise my conclusions. Here they are:

(1) 'Son of man' is a symbol, an apocalyptic counter.

(2) Jesus took it from the book of Daniel. We have good evidence that he knew of the Danielic Son of man, and no reason to think that he knew of any other.

(3) In Daniel 'Son of man' is a symbol standing for 'the people of the saints of the Most High', who are to receive the coming kingdom, with all its benefits, from the hands of the Ancient of Days, i.e. from God himself. There is no Messiah in Daniel.

---

[1] Mark viii. 34–ix. 1. John (vi. 66) tells us that about this time there was a considerable falling off of followers.

[2] Mark viii. 31–3; ix. 30–2; x. 32–4. Cf. ix. 9–13; xiv. 21.

[3] See *The Teaching of Jesus*, pp. 211–34; *Bulletin of the John Rylands Library* XXXII (1950), 171–93.

(4) The 'receiving of the kingdom' is a comprehensive term for the vindication of Israel and the fulfilment of the promises made to the dynasty of David. The 'people of the saints of the Most High' is the actualisation in history of the Israelite ideal. So the Son of man idea in Daniel links the Davidic hope to the Israelite ideal.

(5) The tension between Jesus and his contemporaries, whether friends or opponents, lies in the interpretation of these factors. It can be expressed in two large questions: How does the kingdom come to the Son of man? and, What is the Israelite ideal? For Jesus the answer to both questions is given in its stark simplicity by defining Son of man in terms of the Servant of the Lord portrayed in Isa. xl–lv.

(6) We can see this definition worked out in detail in the words and deeds of the Ministry. In particular, it appears clearly in the sayings about the Son of man, especially those which emphasise his task of service and sacrifice. Along with these go the closely parallel sayings on the task of the disciples and the nature of the power and glory that they may hope to achieve. And finally the definition is completed in the Ministry itself, as a whole and in its several parts.

(7) When these matters are duly weighed it is clear that to say that the Son of man must be the Servant of the Lord is as much as to say that the Messiah must be the Servant of the Lord *par excellence*. But, more than that, Israel must equally be the Servant; or if not all Israel according to the flesh, then those in Israel who will hear and respond to the call. It also appears that the true Israelite ideal is that embodied in the Servant Songs.

(8) This raises a very important point, the question of the relation of the Messiah to Israel and to the Israelite ideal. The answer would seem to be that the Messiah is the embodiment of the true Israelite ideal. This is the positive formulation of what is expressed in negative terms when we talk about the

'sinlessness' of Jesus. The Messiah is also the embodiment of the true Israel. Here we come to the highly important matters comprehended under the term 'corporate personality'. This term is a convenient expression of the fact that in the Semitic mind there is a constant oscillation between the conception of the social group—family, clan, tribe, nation—as an association of individuals in the plural or as a single living social organism about which one can more properly speak in the singular.[1] Where the tendency to think of the social group as a single social organism ('one flesh') is powerful, there is often also a strong tendency to see the corporate personality as embodied or expressed in an individual. The king is apt to be thought of as embodying the corporate personality of his subjects.[2] It is at this point that the transition from Son of man as a name for the people of the saints of the Most High to Son of man as a messianic title becomes possible.

(9) To sum up. The kingdom of God is *God's* kingdom, *God's* reign. That is, it is the actualisation in history of God's power and wisdom as the secret of all true human welfare. The Israelite ideal is a God-given standard. The basic claim of the Gospel is that in Jesus the kingdom of God has come to Israel, the Israelites' God-given ideal is realised. In Jesus Israel (the old or the new Israel) comes into its true kingdom and realises its best ideals.

[1] On this phenomenon see S. A. Cook in *Camb. Anc. Hist.* III, 437–44; and in the third edition of W. Robertson Smith's *Religion of the Semites*, pp. 503 ff., 590 ff., 655 ff.; *The Old Testament; a Reinterpretation*, pp. 115 ff.; H. Wheeler Robinson, 'The Hebrew Conception of Corporate Personality', in *Werden und Wesen des Alten Testaments* (*B.Z.A.W.* 66), pp. 49 ff.; *Inspiration and Revelation in the Old Testament*, pp. 70 f., 81–9, 264; Johs Pedersen, *Israel*; A. R. Johnson, *The One and the Many in the Israelite Conception of God*, pp. 1–17; C. R. North, *The Suffering Servant in Deutero-Isaiah*, pp. 103–10.

[2] Cf. N. A. Dahl, *Das Volk Gottes*, pp. 20 ff.; D. Daube, *Studies in Biblical Law*, pp. 154–89. Something similar may be observed in the Roman Empire in the idea of the Emperor as carrying the person of the State. On this see C. N. Cochrane, *Christianity and Classical Culture*, p. 127; and cf. Seneca, *De Clementia*, I, 4 f. 'tu [Nero] animus rei publicae tuae es, illa corpus tuum.'

As the tension between the intentions of Jesus on the one hand and the hopes of his followers and the fears of his enemies on the other grows more acute, so the Cross becomes more and more clearly the inevitable end of the Ministry. The claims made by Jesus in the period after Caesarea Philippi—claims for the kingdom, not for himself—become more and more absolute. The emphasis is constantly on the price of discipleship rather than on the rewards. The command 'Follow me' takes on a greater and a more tragic urgency. This is reflected in the story of the Transfiguration, an experience which Peter, James and John were allowed to share with Jesus. One very significant feature of the story is the word from Heaven heard by the disciples, 'This is my Son the Beloved, hear him.' 'Hear Him' does not mean merely 'Listen to what he has to say.' It means much more than that: 'Listen to his instructions, and obey.' There is here an unmistakable reference to Deut. xviii. 15 and the promise made to Israel of a prophet like Moses whom God would raise up for them, a prophet whom they must *hear and obey*.[1] The voice of God reinforces the stringent claims of his Son the Beloved.

And the command from Heaven is not superfluous. For we are near the point at which the Galilean Ministry comes to an end and the far more hazardous and heart-breaking enterprise in Judaea and Peraea begins. Jesus determines to go to Jerusalem. It is most important that we should ask why he took this decision, and try to find the right answer to our question. The question has often enough been asked already, and we have a good many answers to choose from. The older lives of Jesus, written from the standpoint of dogmatic

[1] This prophecy was messianically interpreted. See H. J. Schoeps, *Theologie und Geschichte des Judenchristentums*, pp. 87–98; Acts iii. 22 ff.; vii. 37. The Fourth Gospel represents the promise of Deut. xviii. 15 as creating lively, but not necessarily messianic expectations in Jewish minds. Cf. John i. 21; vi. 14; vii. 40. In the first and third of these references the coming prophet is clearly distinguished from the expected Messiah.

orthodoxy, were ready with an answer in terms of orthodox dogmatics. More rationalising studies tended to make the death of Jesus a regrettable incident like the death of Socrates. Jesus goes up to Jerusalem to give a course of lecture-sermons on the Fatherhood of God and the Brotherhood of man, and then becomes the victim of an unfortunate miscarriage of justice. Thoroughgoing eschatology tends to make the Cross an unsuccessful gamble, something like what happens when a chess-player sacrifices his queen in the hope of forcing a mate, and it does not come off. No solution along these lines can give complete satisfaction to heart and mind; and it seems to me that we have a clear hint of the right answer in the facts which we have already considered, above all in the fact of the acute tension between the messianic hopes of the average first-century Jew and the messianic purposes of Jesus. That tension is there, latent but none the less present, from the beginning of the Ministry. It becomes more and more acute as the Ministry progresses. Every day it becomes clearer to the Messiah Jesus, if to nobody else, that the kingdom of God does not come, cannot come, by defeating the kingdoms of the world at their own game; that the Messiah is not, and cannot be, the latest, loudest, and most successful of a long line of international gangsters; that Israel is not to be, and rightly understood cannot be, just another and a greater Rome. But neither Israel nor Rome can see that. Jewish hopes and Roman suspicions are concentrated on the same object, an object far removed from the thoughts of Jesus.

Jesus had discovered and made his own the foundation principle of all thinking about the kingdom of God and of all working for it; a proposition childishly simple and constantly overlooked by the strong and wise, who have it in mind to bring in a kingdom *for* God: *In the kingdom of God God is King.* He had accepted fully all the consequences that follow when this proposition is taken seriously: for example that the messianic task is to be the servant of the Lord *par excellence*; that the servant of the Lord must work in God's way of merciful redemptive love; that he must be the 'friend of publicans and sinners'; that he must proclaim a kingdom of God that is a Ministry of this kind, and cannot be anything else. But to manifest the kingdom of God in this way was almost certainly bound to cool the enthusiasm of the patriotic rank and file, while at the same time it inflamed the fears, suspicions, and enmities of those who sat in the places of power and privilege.

In the light of these considerations we must ask, not, Why did Jesus go up to Jerusalem?, but rather, Is 'going up to Jerusalem' an adequate description of what Jesus did when he left Galilee for the last time? I venture to think that it is not. No doubt Jerusalem is the ultimate goal of the journey; but I think it would be more in keeping with what we know about the mind of Jesus, and also truer to the facts, to say that Jesus left Galilee to continue in the south, that is in Judaea and Peraea, the same kind of Ministry that he had begun in the north. Firstly it accords with what we know about the mind of Jesus. For if one thing has become clear in the course of this inquiry, it is that the kingdom of God, with which Jesus is concerned, is not one that is 'brought in', whether by political action or by any other kind of *coup d'état*. It is a kingdom in which God rules through the messianic Ministry. The kingdom is not something to be added to the Ministry: it is already present in the Ministry. The sacrifice and suffering of the Son of man are not the prelude to triumph: properly understood they are the supreme triumph. From this point of view it is clear that there was nothing more that Jesus could do than just continue his work in the old way in a new area.

Secondly the factual evidence, properly interpreted, supports the view that Jesus left Galilee to continue the messianic

Ministry in Judaea and Peraea. I have set out the arguments for this view in detail elsewhere.[1] I summarise the main points here.

(1) The true text of Mark x. 1 describes not a journey from Galilee to Jerusalem via Peraea, but a ministry in Judaea and Peraea. 'He moved from there [Capernaum, ix. 32] and came into the territories of Judaea and Transjordan; and once more the crowds gathered round him, and he resumed his former practice and took to teaching them.'[2]

(2) There is nothing inherently improbable in the idea of a ministry such as is suggested by Mark x. 1. We have already seen that the headquarters of John the Baptist had been in Peraea; and it is quite possible that Jesus had been associated with John for some time before he opened his own campaign in Galilee after John's arrest. Moreover, there are hints in the Synoptic tradition that Jesus had carried on active work in Judaea before the last stages of the Ministry. It is at least possible that in coming to Judaea and Peraea he was returning to familiar ground and known people.

(3) A good case can be made out for the view that the Cleansing of the Temple took place not at the Passover season but some six months earlier at the time of the Feast of Tabernacles.[3]

If this is so, it becomes possible to make an outline of the

---

[1] *Bulletin of the John Rylands Library*, XXXIII (1951), 271–282.

[2] Reading, καὶ ἐκεῖθεν ἀναστὰς ἔρχεται εἰς τὰ ὅρια τῆς Ἰουδαίας καὶ πέραν τοῦ Ἰορδάνου, καὶ συμπορεύονται πάλιν ὄχλοι πρὸς αὐτόν, καὶ ὡς εἰώθει πάλιν ἐδίδασκεν αὐτούς. The reading of DGΘ, etc. omitting the καί before πέραν, gives a text that reflects the political geography of Palestine in the second century A.D. but not in the time of Jesus. The Byzantine text substitutes διὰ τοῦ for καί before πέραν and is the basis of the common view that Jesus travelled to Judaea via Peraea. The text adopted is that of B and its allies; and it seems clearly superior to the other two.

[3] For the detailed argument see my article in the *Rylands Bulletin*. It is of some interest to observe that Archbishop Carrington's recent study of the structure of Mark in the light of the Jewish and early Christian lectionary systems makes the Cleansing of the Temple and associated incidents fall at the season of Tabernacles rather than Passover.

events in the last year of our Lord's life as follows. The gathering of the five thousand men in the spring of the year about Passover time was followed by Jesus's withdrawal to the districts of Tyre and Sidon and later to the Decapolis. Next comes a second movement to the north via Bethsaida, in the territory of Herod Philip, towards Caesarea Philippi. This is followed by a secret journey through Galilee, ending at Capernaum. The total impression is one of continual movement in and out of Galilee to north and east. Finally comes a movement to the south (Mark x. 1), probably through Samaria into Judaea. A ministry in Judaea and Peraea follows. We must suppose that at some point in it Jesus crossed over into Peraea. The Peraean ministry ended for the time being when Jesus went up to Jerusalem, via Jericho, for the Feast of Tabernacles. On this occasion the Cleansing of the Temple took place. We are then left with a period of some six months (October to April) between the Cleansing of the Temple (Mark xi. 11–25) and the opening of the Passion narrative proper (Mark xiv. 1). This long interval would explain one feature of the Passion story that has always been baffling on the accepted chronology, that is the sudden *volte-face* whereby within a week the enthusiastic crowd shouting Hosannas at the Triumphal Entry is transformed into a howling mob demanding the release of Barabbas and the crucifixion of Jesus. If we are really dealing with two different feasts separated by half a year, the change of attitude can be the more readily explained as due to a growing sense of disappointment and disillusionment caused by the failure of Jesus to lead a great national uprising.

CHAPTER V

THE MESSIANIC MINISTRY: THE PASSION OF THE SON OF MAN

I F the views put forward so far are sound, the last phase of
the Messianic Ministry is really and fully continuous with
what has gone before. The sacrifice of the Son of man is
the logical issue of his service. When Jesus moved from
Galilee to the south, he did not change his purpose or his
methods: he continued his work in the same spirit and manner
as before, but under more hazardous conditions. That he
himself was aware of the hazards and clearly foresaw the
outcome is evident from the fact that he repeatedly fore-
warns the Twelve of the inevitable fate of the Son of man.
These predictions[1] have been a problem to serious students of
the Gospel, if only because of the difficulty of seeing how the
disciples, who had had such clear and ample warning of what
was coming, should have been so completely dumbfounded
when it came. I have suggested as a possible explanation that
they misunderstood the ambiguous term Son of man.[2] They
took it in the familiar collective sense of 'people of the saints
of the Most High' and understood the sayings to mean that
the fight, in which the heathen empire of Rome would be
ousted by the coming kingdom of God, would be a hard
struggle bringing hardship, wounds, and even death to those
who fought on the Lord's side. But the final victory was still

---

[1] Mark viii. 31–3; ix. 30–2; x. 32–4. Cf. ix. 9–13; xiv. 21.
[2] See my article in the *Journal of Ecclesiastical History*, I (1950), 1 ff. I have
stated the arguments in favour of this hypothesis more fully in a paper on
'Realised Eschatology and the Messianic Secret' in a volume of essays in
honour of Professor R. H. Lightfoot.

certain; and when it came, all who had suffered and sacrificed
would be richly rewarded. Those who had given their lives
in the cause would be raised from the dead to take their place
and their share in the New Order. What they were not
prepared for was a tame surrender, followed by the summary
trial and execution of their Messiah.

Jesus, on the other hand, saw the fate of the Son of man
as the fulfilment of the Messianic Ministry; and since the
Messianic Ministry was his task, the destiny of the Son of
man inevitably became his destiny, whether or not anyone
else chose to share it. But the Ministry must go on, and so he
turned southwards.

There are two critical points in the last phase: and they are,
in my view, linked to the two great Jewish festivals: the
Cleansing of the Temple at the Feast of Tabernacles and the
Crucifixion of the Messiah at the Feast of Passover.

First the Cleansing of the Temple. It had been preceded
by the entry of Jesus into the city amid the enthusiastic
hosannas of his followers, who thought they saw the imminent
restoration of 'the kingdom of our father David'.[1] At last
the foreign domination, which they had endured for the
seventy years since Pompey captured Jerusalem, would come
to an end; and the Holy Land would be cleansed from the
polluting presence of the Gentiles. But what happened was
very different. It was the Court of the Gentiles that was
cleansed of intrusive Israelite institutions and activities.
Mark's account[2] of what happened repays careful study.

They came to Jerusalem, and he went into the Temple and
began to turn out all who were carrying on trade within the sacred
precincts. He also overturned the desks of the money-changers
and the seats of the dove-merchants. And he would not allow
anyone to carry any kind of container through the Temple area.
Moreover he told them the reason. He said, 'Is it not stated in

[1] Mark xi. 10.   [2] Mark xi. 15–19.

Scripture: "My House shall be called a house of prayer for all the Gentiles?" But you have made it "a brigand's den".' Now the chief priests and scribes heard this, and they set about finding a way to compass his downfall. For they were afraid of him, because the whole mass of the people were carried away by his teaching. And when evening came, he went away out of the City.

We are accustomed to think of the Cleansing as a drastic exposure and condemnation by Jesus of the exploitation of the Temple worship by the Temple officials for their personal gain. The picture presented by Mark only partly supports this view. He tells us that Jesus began to turn out all those who were buying and selling in the precincts. The terms used are perfectly general, with not the faintest suggestion that the sellers were agents of the Temple authorities, the buyers prospective offerers at the altar, or the merchandise sacrificial animals. The plain words of Mark in their plain meaning present us with something like a general market or exchange, with a good deal of business being transacted besides the official sale of doves and the currency adjustments. These two are mentioned by Mark as a part, and only a part, of the abuses attacked by Jesus. The mention of them is followed by the description of another abuse which our Lord tried to prevent, the use of this court of the Temple as a thoroughfare by messengers and porters. The total impression produced by Mark's account of the matter is that Jesus here confronted a thorough secularisation of the Court of the Gentiles, a secularisation which the Temple authorities may have begun with the money-changing offices and the dove-market, but which had gone very much further than that.

In view of this it is significant that Mark goes on to say καὶ ἐδίδασκεν καὶ ἔλεγεν αὐτοῖς. He made the matter the subject of teaching. This teaching seems to be addressed to all within hearing both 'clerical' and 'lay'. And it certainly looks as if the laity took it better than the clergy.

The essential point is that the Messiah, instead of clearing the Gentiles out of the Holy City, bag and baggage, makes his first public act the vindication of Gentile rights in the Temple itself. For the part of the Temple that was cleansed was the Court of the Gentiles, the one place to which non-Jews had access to worship the God of Israel; and when Jesus cleared away the Jewish traders and business-men, the porters and messengers, he was clearing a space for the Gentiles. This was certainly not in accordance with the accepted Messianic programme.

We are given samples of the kind of reactions provoked by this act of Jesus in the paragraphs of Mark that follow the Cleansing. We have the direct challenge to his authority (xi. 27–33); the trick question about paying taxes to Rome, cleverly designed to put him in the wrong either with the Roman authorities or the Jewish people (xii. 13–17); and the Sadducean problem about the resurrection, doubtless meant to explode his pretensions to be a teacher in Israel (xii. 18–27). We have also what appears to be an honest question, which is given a simple and satisfying answer (xii. 28–34). Here it is significant that the man whom Jesus describes as 'not far from the kingdom of God' is the man who recognises the supremacy of love to God and man as the rule of life.

On Jesus's side we have the recognition, in parabolic form, that the true Messiah need expect no mercy from the Chosen People and their leaders (xii. 1–12); and the final repudiation of the kind of Messiahship for which the people were looking (xii. 35–7).

In all this we can see the growing certainty that Judaea will reject the Messiah and put him to death; and then proceed confidently on the road to ruin and destruction. We have nothing like a complete account of the period from Tabernacles to Passover—we have nothing like a complete account of any period of the Ministry—but we have enough to let us see the way in which events are moving.

With Mark xiv. 1 we come to the Passion narrative proper; and it has a definite time-reference. We are within two days of Passover, and the Jewish leaders are desperately anxious to do away with Jesus, if possible before the feast begins. There had been trouble at the last great festival, Tabernacles; and Passover was a time at which popular feeling was highly excited, and outbreaks of patriotic violence were liable to occur. At this very time, Mark tells us, a strange incident took place at Bethany near Jerusalem. Jesus was having a meal in the house of one Simon, a leper, when a woman[1] came in with a flask of perfumed oil. She broke the flask and poured its contents over the head of Jesus. For the understanding of *her* intention it is relevant to remember that it was apparently not the custom to anoint guests at table during a meal. In reply to criticisms of the extravagance of the act Jesus says that the woman's action is in anticipation of the anointing, which formed part of the preparation of a body for burial. The question of the anointing of dead bodies is an open one: good authorities consider that the New Testament statements are sufficient evidence for the existence of the custom.[2] When Jesus said that she had anointed his body in advance for the burial, he may have meant that she had done a gracious act a short while before it would be actually needed. He may also have meant that her action had made his death inevitable. This latter interpretation becomes very likely if there is, as I believe, a real parallel between this story and the incident narrated in II Kings ix. 1–13. There, in like circumstances, Jehu is anointed king of Israel. It may well

[1] In Mark the woman is completely anonymous. Later identifications of her with Mary Magdalene, Mary the sister of Martha, and the 'woman that was a sinner' in the story in Luke vii, are works of pious imagination.

[2] See Billerbeck, *Kommentar*, II, 53; Krauss, *Talm. Arch.* II, 55; D. Daube, *Anglican Theol. Rev.* XXXII (1950), 189, n. 19.

be that the woman in Bethany thought that she was anointing the Messianic King.[1] Whether she thought so or not, the news that Jesus had been anointed in Bethany would be a serious matter if it leaked out; and once it came to the ears of the authorities, it could easily be a hanging matter. It is all the more significant that the story of the anointing is placed by Mark between his account of the Jewish authorities in search of some way to destroy Jesus and his story of the visit of Judas to them. It is easily conceivable that what Judas revealed to them was the fact that the anointing had taken place. If so the visit of Judas gave them definite evidence that the dangers they feared were real dangers, as well as a real chance of getting rid of Jesus in time. The anointing and the visit of Judas appear to belong to the Wednesday of the last week of Jesus's life.

On the Thursday evening of the same week Jesus shared a meal with his disciples. It is still an open question whether or not it was the Jewish Passover meal:[2] we know it, in the light of what followed, simply as the Last Supper. After the meal the company went away to a garden, called Gethsemane, outside the City. There Jesus was arrested by the Temple police. They were guided to the spot by Judas Iscariot, one of the Twelve. What Judas did, and what the Gospels mean to tell us that he did, was to make it possible for the authorities to seize Jesus secretly: that is, he made it possible for them to use gestapo methods rather than honest police methods. An open arrest in Jerusalem in daylight might well have caused

---

[1] This is the view of Dibelius (*Jesus*, p. 82), who says that the woman saw in Jesus 'der König des Gottesreiches'.

[2] The uncertainty on this point goes right back into the Gospel tradition itself. Mark certainly appears to understand that the Last Supper was a Passover meal: the Fourth Gospel is quite explicit that it was not, and that the death of Christ took place at the time when the Passover lambs were being slaughtered. The Johannine tradition may claim some support from remarks made by St Paul in I Cor. For a very full discussion of the problem see J. Jeremias, *Die Abendmahlsworte Jesu*, 2nd ed.

a riot. What Judas sold to the chief priests was his inside knowledge of the place where Jesus and his disciples would be that night. This act can only be described as a betrayal. There has been a good deal of conjecture about the possible motives for this dreadful act. If the triumphal entry and the cleansing of the Temple are put back to the time of Tabernacles it is perhaps a little easier to suppose that the action of Judas arose out of the bitter disillusionment of a fanatical Jewish patriot, as he contemplated what appeared to him as six months of spineless inaction, after the splendid opportunity of the triumphal entry had been mishandled by an unprovoked attack on the Jerusalem sanctuary instead of decisive action against the Roman oppressor. However that may be, we are left with the hard fact that the other disciples could find no excuse for Judas, and that Jesus himself could only say, 'Alas for the man by whom the Son of man is betrayed: it would have been better for him if he had never been born.'

The arrangements for the arrest had been made with some care to ensure that whatever else happened Jesus himself should not escape. The arrangements worked: the disciples got away, but Jesus was held. He was taken under escort to the high priest's house. Peter followed as far as the house; but, when challenged by the servants, he denied all knowledge of his Master.

The proceedings before the Sanhedrin should not be regarded as a formal trial, but rather as an informal inquiry. Nevertheless, though the Sanhedrin was sitting, so to speak, in committee rather than in open court, the proceedings were a matter of life and death to the accused. By the time they were over two things had happened: first the members of the Sanhedrin had made up their minds definitely and finally that Jesus was a menace to them and their people and that he should be put to death; and secondly, he had delivered himself into their hands by admitting openly that he regarded himself as the Messiah. By doing this he made it possible for them to bring him before the Roman governor on a capital charge.[1]

Early on Friday morning Jesus was taken to Pilate's headquarters in Jerusalem and the information was laid against him. The Governor was not greatly impressed by the case. His private opinion seems to have been that the whole affair arose out of the malice and ill-will of the Jewish authorities, and that he was being used for their purposes. There his judgement was sound. He also came to the conclusion, after seeing Jesus and questioning him, that he was harmless. He even made some abortive efforts to dismiss the charge or to give Jesus a pardon. But the accusers were insistent and their arguments were backed by the demonstrations of a crowd of 'loyal' Jews assembled for the purpose. A decision had to be given. Life was cheap in those days. There was a case of sorts; and even if Jesus was practically harmless alive, he would be quite harmless dead. So sentence was passed and execution followed without delay. By sunset on Friday it was over; and Jesus, with all the hopes and fears he had aroused, was buried in the rock tomb.

And most of the people who had been concerned doubtless went to bed that night with fairly easy consciences. Pilate had earned another day's salary as Procurator of Judaea; and his province was quiet and peaceful—at any rate on the surface. The Temple authorities could feel that they had made things secure against untimely reforming zeal—for the time being at least. Patriotic Jews could tell themselves that it had been a mistake ever to imagine that Jesus was the kind of leader they were looking for—and in that they were not mistaken. Devout Jews could reflect that such an end as that

[1] The fact that it was possible to do this, and the fact that the Roman statement of the case was 'Jesus of Nazareth, king of the Jews', is eloquent commentary on the nature of the Jewish messianic hope in this period.

which had overtaken Jesus was hardly to be wondered at, after the way in which he had flouted the scribes and even criticised the provisions of the Law itself. We might almost say that Jesus was crucified with the best intentions; and that those who sent him to the Cross believed that they were doing their plain duty by the Empire or the Temple, or the Law or the hope of Israel. Doubtless many, perhaps most, of them did so believe.

But Jesus stood for something greater than the Empire or the Temple or the Law. He stood for the kingdom of God. In truth he was the kingdom of God. In his Ministry he had shown the rule of God in action, what it offers to men everywhere and what it demands from them. In Pilate, Caiaphas, and the rest the lesser loyalties united against the kingdom of God incarnate in Jesus the Messiah; and so Jesus went to the Cross—and made it his everlasting throne.

CHAPTER VI

THE RISEN CHRIST AND THE MESSIANIC SUCCESSION

WHEN Pilate had the notice 'Jesus of Nazareth, king of the Jews' tacked up on the Cross, he no doubt thought that there was another false coin nailed to the counter. And in their several spheres the Jewish authorities also felt that they had disposed of something false and dangerous. What had they all been trying to do? The only possible answer is that they had been trying to put a stop to what we call the Ministry, and what they would have called the subversive activities or the dangerous teaching or the pernicious influence of this false prophet or bogus Messiah from Nazareth. (After all, it was well known that you could not expect any good out of Galilee.)

There are many uncertainties to be reckoned with in tracing the history of Jesus and the early Church, but here is one certainty: the Ministry of Jesus was not stopped. The Roman and Jewish authorities had hardly begun to congratulate themselves on having dealt with another crisis in a statesman-like way, when the crisis was upon them again in a new form. The disciples, cowed and dispirited, had hardly begun to ask themselves what they should do next or where they could safely go, when the answer was given to them in the way they least expected. The Crucified was alive again and active among them. From the first Easter Sunday onwards the recurrent refrain in the talk of the disciples, whether among themselves or in their contact with others, is, 'He is risen', 'God has raised him from the dead.' It is the resurrection of Jesus that is asserted and believed, not the immortality of souls, including the soul of Jesus.

89

It is therefore important that we should be clear about what the word 'Resurrection' meant in New Testament times. It had nothing whatever to do with the survival of disembodied spirits in some heavenly sphere. On the contrary, it was essentially a restoration to life *in this world*, a bringing back of the dead person from the cold and shadowy underworld to resume his place among his kinsfolk and friends and to recover the health and vigour that were his before he died. Even if the conditions of existence are supposed to have been drastically changed before the resurrection takes place, it is recognisably the same person who returns to rejoin people, who will recognise him. And however much the conditions may have changed, it is assumed that there will be a real continuity of purpose and activity between the new life and the old, just as there is a real continuity of personality between the man who died and the man who returns to life. The nearest thing in our ordinary experience to the Jewish and early Christian idea of death and resurrection is falling asleep and waking up; and it is a very significant fact that the first unmistakable reference to the resurrection of the dead in the Old Testament[1] is made in terms of sleeping and waking: 'And many of them that *sleep* in the dust of the earth shall *awake*, some to everlasting life, and some to shame and everlasting contempt.' And equally, when there is no expectation of a resurrection the natural way to express it is in terms of a sleep from which there is no awaking:

> Man lieth down and riseth not:
> Till the heavens be no more, they shall not awake,
> Nor be roused out of their sleep.[2]

Now one of the standing wonders of life is just the fact that when I come out of oblivion any fine morning, I am at

---

[1] Dan. xii. 2. Cf. II Kings ix. 31; Jer. li. 39, 57; Job xiv. 12 (all negative); Isa. xxvi. 19 (positive).
[2] Job xiv. 12.

once aware that I am the same person that lived in my home yesterday and went to sleep there last night. The task I left unfinished yesterday is still there, still *my* task, and I can take it up where I left off. The plans I was making yesterday are still there waiting for further consideration and elaboration. This continuity of personality and life is a great marvel; and it is only excessive familiarity with it that hides its wonder from us. When we try to think of death and resurrection, as the first Christians thought of them, we cannot do better than think in terms of sleeping and waking, and the wonderful way in which the self contrives every night to leap the dark gulf of unconsciousness and arrive safely on the other side complete with all its hopes and fears, joys and sorrows, memories of the past and plans for the future.

It is a corollary to this that when people seek for evidences of the immortality of the soul they tend to find satisfaction either in philosophical arguments, of which the *Phaedo* is a magnificent example, or in alleged communications from the spirit world. Evidences of resurrection must needs be more closely connected with this world; and that is the case with the evidences for the resurrection of Jesus.

It is usual, and correct, to say that the New Testament evidences for the resurrection fall into two classes: those which report the finding of the empty tomb, and those which report appearances of the Lord to various people. It is possible to accept both classes, or one (in that case the appearances of the Lord are likely to be preferred to the stories of the empty tomb), or neither. If you take the last option, you are at once rid of all problems except one—that of providing some explanation for the most gigantic and successful swindle in human history. Let us look at the evidence.

The first written record is I Cor. xv. 1–11. It is obviously and explicitly a report of what Paul had preached in Corinth some years earlier. And Paul had 'received' it earlier still.

He links it up with his own conversion experience. And I should surmise that it may well have been one of the things he talked about with Peter, when the two men met in Jerusalem[1] some twenty years before I Corinthians was written. It is worth noting that in the catalogue of witnesses given by Paul the name of Peter stands first and his own name last. The appearance of the risen Lord was an experience common to both men; and if our guess is right, the first witness and the last, on Paul's list, were comparing their experiences within about five years of having them.

Further, we may note that Paul bases his apostleship on this personal experience which he had had on the road to Damascus. When we read the Corinthian letters and Galatians, we tend to think that what Paul is chiefly concerned about is the defence of his own status as an official of the Church ranking with Peter and John and James the Lord's brother; and there is much in the tone and temper of these letters to lend colour to that view. But is that the whole truth? The better one comes to know Paul, the clearer it is that by far the most important thing in the world to him was his life's work, his missionary task, the task which he regarded as his supreme privilege. What he says, therefore, in I Cor. xv. 9 f., is of the utmost importance because it directly links his apostolic *task* with his experience of the Risen Lord. In doing so it gives us good warrant for believing that the account in Acts xxvi. 15–20 gives a substantially accurate report of what happened when Paul saw and heard the Risen Christ and was turned from an ardent opponent of the work of Christ into the most ardent of workers for and under Christ. The vital point is that here, in the one case where we have the first-hand testimony of a man who claimed to have seen the Risen Lord, that experience is inextricably linked with a command and a commission to work for Christ under Christ's direction.

[1] Gal. i. 18.

But Paul's case is not unique. The other stories of resurrection appearances tell the same tale. In the Fourth Gospel we have what is sometimes called the recommissioning of Peter:[1] 'Feed my sheep.' In Matthew we have the great generalisation of all the particular experiences in xxviii. 19. And similar things appear in Luke xxiv and Acts i. Indeed it is hardly too much to say that the one constant feature in all the recorded experiences of this kind in the first days of the Church is this settled conviction that Jesus himself is alive and active, continuing *his* Ministry through his disciples.

So far I have said nothing about Mark, our earliest Gospel and a prime authority in our reconstruction of the story of the Ministry. When we turn to Mark we come face to face with a much-debated problem. It may be taken as certain that Mark xvi. 9–20 in the Authorised Version is not genuine, and that the alternative endings which appear in certain manuscripts are also spurious. All that we have from Mark's own hand ends at xvi. 8 with the words ἐφοβοῦντο γάρ, 'for they were afraid'. Is that all that Mark wrote? Some excellent scholars hold that it is.[2] I cannot agree, and I take this opportunity of trying again to find a solution of the problem.

Let us begin by asking what Mark has told us in xvi. 1–8. Three women, Mary Magdalene, Mary the mother of James, and Salome, buy unguents and come to the tomb for the anointing, arriving very early on Sunday morning. While they are debating how to get the tomb opened, they notice that it is already open, the large stone slab which acted as a door having been rolled back. On going into the recess they find a 'young man' in white sitting there and are terrified by the sight.[3] The

[1] John xxi. 15–23.
[2] For an admirable statement of the case for the ending at xvi. 8, see R. H. Lightfoot, *The Gospel Message of St Mark*.
[3] The verb used, ἐξεθαμβήθησαν, implies the terror that is aroused by the supernatural. It is a very much stronger expression than the ἐφοβοῦντο of verse 8.

THE RISEN CHRIST AND

young man reassures them and says, 'You are looking for Jesus of Nazareth who had been crucified. He has been raised (from the dead). He is not here. Here is the place where they laid him. But (ἀλλά) go and tell his disciples and Peter (in particular), "He is leading the way for you into Galilee; you will see him there as he told you."'[1]

On receiving the message from the 'young man' the women ran out and away from the tomb 'beside themselves with terror'.[2] And they said nothing to anybody, for they were afraid (ἐφοβοῦντο). There are many questions to be asked. Of what were they afraid? Why were they afraid? What did they not tell to anybody? And why?

Now in Luke xxiv. 22–4 we have an independent story. There the two disciples on the way to Emmaus tell the stranger who has joined them that 'certain women of our number surprised us greatly. They had been early at the tomb, failed to find the body, and came back with the story that they had had a vision of angels, who told them that he was alive. So some of our people went off to the tomb and found things there as the women had described them; but they did not see him.' If we give any credence to this account—and I know of no good reason why we should not—the women did tell about all that had happened to them, except one thing. *They did not deliver the message which had been entrusted to them; because they were afraid.*

And they had good reason to be afraid, afraid in the simple ordinary sense of the word. The only safety, as it then seemed, for themselves and their friends was to lie low. And it is

---

[1] 'As he told you' is a clear reference back to xiv. 28, where, after the Last Supper, Jesus had told the Twelve that they would all be completely disillusioned about him in accordance with the Old Testament text which said, 'I will smite the shepherd, and the sheep will be scattered' (Zech. xiii. 7). 'But,' he had added, 'after I am raised (from the dead) I will lead the way for you into Galilee.'

[2] εἶχεν γὰρ αὐτὰς τρόμος καὶ ἔκστασις. Again a very strong expression in sharp contrast to the ἐφοβοῦντο which follows.

common knowledge that there is no better hiding-place than a big city. To return to Galilee would be fatal, with Antipas waiting there to liquidate the remnants of the Nazarene movement. Here we have a sufficient motive for their failure to deliver the message and a sufficient explanation of their fear.

We can now go a step further. The non-delivery of the message is imperatively required to account for the fact that the disciples and Peter did not go to Galilee and that our most reliable traditions represent the main resurrection appearances as taking place in and about Jerusalem, and the main headquarters of the Christian community as being established there and not in Galilee.

I should therefore draw the conclusion that, whether or not Mark wrote anything after xvi. 8 (and I find it less difficult to suppose that he wrote something now lost than that he was unable or unwilling to finish the job), what he did write up to xvi. 8 points forward quite definitely to a continuation in which the disciples did not go to Galilee because they had not been told, and consequently the resurrection appearances took place in and about Jerusalem. Further the undelivered message, 'He is leading the way for you', is a plain indication of what the appearances are concerned with. There are three points.

The first is continuing leadership. We are already familiar, from the story of the Ministry, with the picture of Jesus leading the way and the disciples following on behind sometimes with courage and confidence, sometimes in perplexity and apprehension, but still following. The message to the disciples from the empty tomb tells them that the leadership they have known and learned to rely on continues and will continue.

The second point is that this continuing leadership is leadership in a continuing Ministry. The Risen Lord, as it were, picks up the threads of his work among the oppressed and neglected, the sick and the sinful, in the same kind of way that we all get up in the morning and begin another day's work linked up with what we were doing yesterday. There are differences, of course, in the case of the Resurrection. The Gospel narratives let us understand that the Risen Christ is freed from some of the limitations that hampered him in the first phase of his Ministry, as they hamper us in our work: for example, the notorious difficulty, which even the telephone and television only partly overcome, of being in two or more places at the same time. But these features of the story, interesting and important though they are, should not be allowed to divert our attention from the central fact that *the work taken up again by the Risen Lord is the work of the earthly Ministry*, strengthened, intensified, enlarged, no doubt, but still in all essentials the same tasks, informed by the same spirit and directed to the same ends. The Risen Christ still 'has compassion on the multitudes', is still 'the friend of publicans and sinners', still 'comes to give service rather than to receive it', still 'seeks and saves the lost'. And we are meant to understand that the doing of these things is the supreme task and the highest honour in the world; and that the doing of them as Christ does them is the true revelation of the glory of God.

The third point which emerges from the study of the Resurrection narratives is that Jesus continues to delegate his work to others. It is clear from the Gospel records that when Jesus first gathered a group of disciples round him, he had a definite plan in mind. It had two phases, one in which the disciples should 'be with him', learning his ways by seeing him· at work, another in which 'he would send them out' to do the kind of work that he himself was doing, in his way and in his spirit. This delegation of the 'work of the Ministry' is an essential part of it; and we read of two occasions on which groups of delegates (or apostles) were sent out by

Jesus. Now one of the most impressive features of the Resurrection narratives is that they show the Risen Lord doing the same thing. The Gospels of Matthew, Luke and John all represent him instructing the disciples to continue the tasks they had already begun during the Ministry. It is true that the message which they will now deliver is vastly enriched and deepened by the experiences through which they have lately passed; but it is still of a piece with the things they had been taught from the beginning of their discipleship. It is true that the service they are called upon to render takes on new meaning in the light of the Cross but it is still of a piece with the things that Jesus showed them when first they attached themselves to him.

We are not confined to the Gospels for evidence of this point. St Paul, who presents himself as a witness to the Resurrection as one to whom the Lord had appeared, makes it clear that when Christ spoke to him on the Damascus road it was to give him his orders; and we know how promptly Paul responded to the challenge, and how faithfully he served his new Master for the rest of his life.

And I said, 'Who art thou, Lord?' And the Lord said, 'I am Jesus whom thou persecutest. But arise, and stand upon thy feet; for to this end have I appeared unto thee, to appoint thee a minister and a witness, both of the things wherein thou hast seen me, and of the things wherein I will appear unto thee; delivering thee from the people and from the Gentiles, unto whom I send thee, to open their eyes, that they may turn from darkness to light, and from the power of Satan unto God, that they may receive remission of sins and an inheritance among them that are sanctified by faith in me.' Wherefore, O King Agrippa, I was not disobedient unto the heavenly vision. (Acts xxvi, 15–19.)

In this conception of the Risen Christ continuing his Ministry through the agency of his disciples we begin to impinge upon the Pauline doctrine of the Church as the Body of Christ, the continuation of the Incarnation. For my own part I should be strongly inclined to say 'the working body of Christ' rather than 'the mystical body of Christ', the working body which is the continuation of the Messianic Ministry. The Ministry has gone on for nineteen centuries and more; and it still goes on. What is the secret of its staying-power? The answer of the whole New Testament is that it is the Risen Christ himself who is carrying it out. It is very easy for us, who have been brought up in a scientific age, to think of Jesus bequeathing his principles and ideals to his followers and leaving it to them to take up and carry on the task he is presumed to have laid down somewhere about A.D. 30. That is not the New Testament picture at all. There can be little doubt that if it had been left to the disciples to take up tasks, their choice would have fallen elsewhere. Simon Peter and Andrew would have spent the rest of their unrecorded lives trying to build up again the prosperous fishing business which they had so rashly abandoned to join the ill-fated prophet of Nazareth. And the others likewise. No: the secret of the matter is that it is Christ who picks up the threads, Christ who takes the lead, Christ whose presence and power are constant inspiration and strength. The Resurrection means above all just this, that *Christians do not inherit their task from Christ, they share it with him*. We are not the successors of Jesus, but his companions. That is the measure both of our privilege and our responsibility. The essential nature of the Church is that so long as the world endures there should be in the world an organism which is truly responsive to the motions and impulses of Christ's mind and heart and will, an organism completely expendable in the carrying out of his purposes.

The things I have been trying to say are summed up for us in the closing words of St Matthew's Gospel. 'And Jesus came to them and spoke to them, saying, "All authority has been given to me in heaven and on earth. Go therefore and make disciples of all nations, baptising them into the name of the Father and of the Son and of the Holy Spirit, teaching them to observe all the things that I have commanded you. And lo I am with you always, even to the end of the world." ' Here is a Risen Christ who comes in full power to resume his work in the world; who takes the lead among his followers and sends them out on his errands; who links the work they are about to begin with his work that he himself initiated; above all, who assures his disciples of his own abiding presence with them. The secret of the Church's achievement lies in this formula. But the formula is itself the record of a great and transforming experience of being recalled to a task by a known and trusted Master: the discovery that they were to work on under him, for him, and with him, as of old; above all, the assurance that nothing could break this association: 'Lo I am with you always, even unto the end of the world.'

INDEX OF NAMES AND SUBJECTS

INDEX OF NAMES AND SUBJECTS

INDEX OF REFERENCES

INDEX OF REFERENCES

INDEX OF REFERENCES